Understanding Families

Critical Thinking and Analysis

William Egelman

Iona College

Boston   New York   San Francisco
Mexico City   Montreal   Toronto   London   Madrid   Munich   Paris
Hong Kong   Singapore   Tokyo   Cape Town   Sydney

Executive Editor: *Jeff Lasser*
Editor in Chief: *Karen Hanson*
Editorial Assistant: *Andrea Christie*
Marketing Manager: *Krista Groshong*
Editorial Production Service: *Chestnut Hill Enterprises, Inc.*
Manufacturing Buyer: *JoAnne Sweeney*
Cover Administrator: *Kristina Mose-Libon*
Electronic Composition: *Omegatype Typography, Inc.*

For related titles and support materials, visit our online catalogue at
www.ablongman.com.

Copyright © 2004, Pearson Education, Inc.
All rights reserved. No part of the material protected by this copyright notice
may be reproduced or utilized in any form or by any means, electronic or
mechanical, including photocopying, recording, or by any information storage
and retrieval system, without written permission from the copyright owner.

To obtain permission(s) to use material from this work, please submit a written
request to Allyn and Bacon, Permissions Department, 75 Arlington Street,
Boston, MA 02116 or fax your request to 617-848-7320.

Between the time Website information is gathered and then published, some
sites may have closed. Also, the transcription of URLs can result in typographical
errors. The publisher would appreciate notification where these occur so that
they may be corrected in subsequent editions.

Library of Congress Cataloging-in-Publication Data
Egelman, William.
    Understanding families : critical thinking and analysis / William Egelman.
        p.   cm.
    Includes bibliographical references and index.
    ISBN 0-205-35262-6
        1. Family.   2. Family—United States.   I. Title.
    HQ515.E44 2004
306.85—dc21

                                                    2003040317

Printed in the United States of America
    10 9 8 7 6 5 4 3 2 1   08 07 06 05 04 03

Contents

Preface

All the students I have taught over the past thirty years in my Sociology of the Family courses have directly and indirectly contributed to this work. This is because this type of course tends to stimulate students to be forthcoming about their own personal experiences. I have learned a great deal about the diversity of family life from them.

A number of students worked with a rough draft of the exercises in the Analysis sections of this book. I appreciate their comments and suggestions. I would like to recognize their contributions by name: Katherine Calabro, Brian Cesario, Renee Eger, Cristina Fata, Talia Gallardo, Daniela Gurriero, Yaritza Maldonado, Jamie Pleva, Jonathan Remeny, Alissa Sangounchitte, Kercise Sanlouis, Irene Scalera, Toni-Ann Scherer, Sara Sgrizzi, Natalie Wiedemann, and Laura Zecchin.

My own family experiences have, of course, influenced my perception of family life in general. My parents, Joseph and Rose Egelman, both now deceased, were immigrants. They certainly were not perfect, but they were kind and loving. They created a nurturing environment within which they raised three sons. My brothers, both older than I, were my protectors and served as models for me. As we grew older we grew even closer and I came to appreciate them as my brothers and as individuals in their own right. I mourn the loss of my older brother, Jay, who died several years ago, but I cherish his memory and still enjoy a wonderful camaraderie with my surviving brother, Abe. My sisters-in-law are more like blood relatives than in-laws. The same holds true for my wife's mother and sister.

As for my own family, there is not a day that goes by when I do not learn something new about family life. In the movie *Parenthood,* directed by Ron Howard, Steve Martin plays a father who is somewhat overwhelmed by the challenges posed by his own family. His mother-in-law suggests that some people like to live their life on a carousel—it just goes around and around. Others, however, prefer a roller coaster with its ups and downs and all the excitement one experiences from that type of ride. I think the screenwriter was referring to my family. Thanks for the ride!

Introduction

I have taught classes in the Sociology of Family for thirty years. I do not make this statement in order to show off my expertise. In the thirty years I have taught this class, what we call the family has undergone remarkable change. In fact I tell my students that change should be seen as an underlying theme for the entire course. It is not just the change by itself that is remarkable; it is also the speed of the change. For college students, thirty years may seem like an eternity; most of my students are barely twenty when they take my course, but in historical time thirty years is a mere snap of the fingers.

At times I am overwhelmed by the changes I have witnessed, and it is sometimes difficult to communicate to students the real nature of these changes. In many ways this book is written to help me and, hopefully, other professors and their students come to some understanding of the changes that have occurred. Each chapter begins with a brief essay that discusses the major ideas, including my own point of view, on the topics covered. The second part of each chapter has an analysis section. This section will give students the opportunity to examine and analyze data relevant to the subject being discussed. Every analysis section includes at least some **longitudinal data**, data that covers some span of time. By having students analyze these data, I hope that they too will gain some sense of the degree of change that has occurred in the recent past.

Let's look at some of the changes in family life over the past thirty years. (Each of these will be discussed in much greater depth in the relevant chapters.) First, let us look at marriage. In 1970, for people twenty-five to twenty-nine years old, 85 percent were married. Put another way, close to nine out of ten people were married prior to their thirtieth birthday. Today, only 55 percent of people in their late twenties have been married. Almost half of all people in their late twenties have yet to marry.

This change in marriage can also be examined by looking at the **median** age at which people marry. The median is the midpoint in a series of numbers. In 1970, the median age for marriage for men was 23.2 years; for women it was 20.8. If we look only at the female number, that means that, for all women who married, 50 percent married before their twenty-first birthday. I relate this information to my female students and I am amazed at their reaction. They cannot seem to fathom how any woman could marry so young. Their reaction speaks volumes to me about the shift in attitudes toward marriage, and what women now see as the appropriate time to marry. This is borne out by the current data on median age for marriage. It has increased for both men and women: for men it is now almost twenty-seven years, and for women the figure is twenty-five years. The fact that the median age for marriage for women has gone from twenty-one to twenty-five in thirty years may not seem to be a dramatic change. From a sociological and historical perspective, however, it is an extraordinary increase in a relatively short period of time.

Another change has been in labor force participation—the number of people working or actively looking for work. In the past thirty years the number of women in the labor force has more than doubled; the actual increase is 112 percent. During the same time male labor force participation rates also increased, but only by 47 percent. In 1970 there were almost two male workers for every female worker. Today that ratio is almost even.

A third area of change is the divorce rate. It is no secret that divorce has increased substantially over the past thirty years. Divorce is one of the most written about and discussed and debated issues in our society: the number of divorces has more than tripled in the past thirty years. (The chapter on divorce will explore this issue in much greater depth.) Connected with divorce are the living arrangements of children. In 1970 about one out of ten children were living with a single parent (divorced, never-married, or widowed); today it is a little over one out of four children. Some experts project that half of all children alive today will spend at least part of their childhood living with one parent.

A fourth change is the number of persons who live together without being married. This pattern has increased at least threefold over the past thirty years, with some data indicating that the increase is more likely to be fivefold. Living together, nonmarital cohabitation, unmarried couples—whatever this lifestyle is called—the number of people living together without being married has increased dramatically. It is one example of a larger trend toward a diversity of family lifestyles that exist in the United States today. Another trend is the increase in interracial marriages. While still constituting a small percentage of all marriages, black–white intermarriages have gone from 65,000 in 1970 to 330,000 in 1998. This is a fivefold increase in one generation. There have also been increases in other types of intermarriage as well. All of these changes barely expose the overall change in family structures and patterns. This book will help the reader explore these and other changes that have occurred and are still occurring today.

How should one approach the reading of this book, and to a larger degree the study of the sociology of the family? Many years ago I took a graduate course in the Sociology of the Family and I will never forget what the professor said the first evening class was held. He said that in order to understand sociologically the nature of family, we have to make believe that we just arrived from Mars. We know nothing of the Homo Sapien family system. His point, of course, was the need for us to be objective in our study of family life.

I often tell my students that teaching a course on the family is both the easiest course to teach and, at the same time, the most difficult. It is easy because everyone has some experience in families. Each student has some knowledge and experience participating in family life. But this also poses a problem, the problem of objectivity. I can tell that some points I make in class are very familiar to my students. In fact sometimes they come up to me after a lecture, and say that it sounded like I know their family personally. However, on other occasions, they come to me and say that I made no sense at all. That is, they do not know any family that is similar to what I had just lectured on in class. The same may hold true for this book. It illustrates the point my professor made some years ago. We know our family but we do not know all families. Keep that in mind as you read these essays and do the analyses.

One last point before you begin to read this book. Sociology, ideally, strives to be objective in its approach to studying the family. I, as a professional sociologist, strive to do the same. This is what makes sociology a particularly difficult endeavor. We study human behavior and we are human. Although I hate to admit it, my own personal history influences how I approach any subject matter. My parents, brothers, and childhood experiences all help shaped who I am and how I do my sociology. None of us is immune to our own upbringing. Keep this in mind when you undertake the analysis sections of these chapters. Understand that, just like me, each of you is the product of your own experiences, especially, I believe, the experiences in family life.

1

Is the Family Universal? International Family Comparisons

Families exist in all cultures. Therefore, the answer to the questions posed in the title of the chapter is "yes." However, the types of families may vary from culture to culture, and even within cultures. Anthropologists and sociologists have spent a great deal of time studying the similarities and differences between family systems.

During the eighteenth and nineteenth centuries, many European social scientists, missionaries, and others traveled to other parts of the world and studied the peoples in those regions. Many of these European observers carried with them **ethnocentric** beliefs. **Ethnocentrism** is the belief that your culture is superior to all other cultures. Any culture that has different customs and beliefs would be viewed as less civilized. Many of these observers studied other cultures and their accompanying family systems through the lens of European values and beliefs. Those cultures that had family systems different from the Western and European model were viewed as savage or barbaric.

With the development of the social sciences in the latter part of the nineteenth century, a new way of looking at cultures emerged. This new approach is **cultural relativism**. This approach demanded that the observer look at elements of a culture within the context of the culture being studied. In other words, do not permit your own personal values and beliefs, those that come from the culture within which you were raised, to influence the analysis of cultural elements. More specifically, if one is studying the family systems of, let us say Australians, the observer should study the family system within the context of the larger Australian society. Questions such as: what factors led to the emergence of a particular family form, how do the powerful groups in society support or undermine family systems, what are the functions of the family within the society, and how do persons in families come to define their roles are all questions that researchers may focus on in their study of Australian families.

Social scientists quickly became aware of the great diversity that exists in family systems around the world. In addition, it became apparent that diverse family systems existed within cultures as well. Social scientists developed a vocabulary to help describe and analyze these differences.

There are two basic family types. The **nuclear family** is made up of one or two generations consisting of relations by blood or marriage. This category includes husband–wife marriages with or without children and mother–child or father–child families. **Extended families** are more than one nuclear family that may share a household and/or economic resources. The extended family can be vertical, including grandparents, parents, and grandchildren, horizontal, made up of married brothers and/or sisters, or some combination of the two.

There are two major marital forms, monogamy and polygamy. **Monogamy** requires people to be married to one person at a time. Today, given current rates of divorce and remarriage, a number of people have more than one spouse in their lifetime, but not at the same time. This is referred to as **serial monogamy. Polygamy** allows for more than one spouse at the same time. Historically, more societies have allowed for polygamy than the other marital forms. There are two subforms of polygamy. **Polygyny** allows a husband to have more than one wife at the same time; **polyandry** allows a wife to have more than one husband at the same time. The rarest marital form is polyandry. In those few societies that have a polyandrous system, it usually involves a woman marrying a man and all his brothers. This is called fraternal polyandry.

All of these forms, however, are **norms.** Norms constitute what is permitted or expected in a society. Marital norms are what a society allows for or expects in terms of marriage. Historically, most marriages have probably been monogamous, even in polygamous societies. The major reason for this is that most men, regardless of the society in which they live, could not afford more than one wife.

In addition to these basic terms, in the sociology of the family there are also a series of terms that use the prefixes **patri-** or **matri-.** Any term beginning with *patri-* refers to the male line, and any term beginning with *matri-* refers to the female line.

Let's look at three examples. If we add the suffix *-local* to *patri-* or *matri-* we get **patrilocal** and **matrilocal.** These terms refer to where a couple lives when they get married. In patrilocal societies the newlyweds live with the groom's family, and in a matrilocal society the newlyweds live with the bride's family. In the United States, we have what is termed **neolocal residence:** the newlyweds set up their own independent households.

A second pair of terms refers to lineage: **patrilineal** and **matrilineal.** In creating a family tree, which side of the family is dominant? In patrilineal societies the male line is the significant ancestry that determines the place individuals occupy in the social system. In matrilineal societies it is the female line that serves the function of social placement. In the United States, there is a variation called **bilateral descent** in which both sides of the family tree have equal influence in the individual's social placement.

The third pair of terms refer to the relative power women and men have in a society. **Patriarchy** and **matriarchy** refer to power relations in society. In patriarchal societies, males hold positions of power both within the family and within the larger societal structures (government, economy, etc.). Matriarchal societies are dominated by females.

Although this issue has been debated in various intellectual circles, there is no substantial evidence for the existence of matriarchies. This does not justify patriarchy. It simply means that there is no historical evidence that women have ruled in any society. It is true that some women have risen to positions of great power in the United States and elsewhere, and certainly the role of women in a number of societies is changing, but the fact remains that matriarchy is more a myth than historical fact. Within societies there are certainly families that are matriarchal, but this is not the norm.

Some believe that we have an **egalitarian system** in the United States. This involves an equal distribution of power both within the family and within society. Again, this may be seen as a norm. The reality may be something different. For example, let us look at an everyday symbolic illustration of patriarchy. When a woman and man marry, in most cases the woman takes the man's last name. In some cases, a woman may hyphenate her maiden name or use it as a new middle name. Some women do maintain their maiden name after marriage, but that does yet appear to be the norm. One should also remember that the woman's maiden name was her father's name, not her mother's name at birth.

In reviewing these various terms, one may begin to grasp the potential diversity of family systems that exists in the world. In looking at the terms, remember that there may be a variety of combinations and configurations. For example, a given family system might be both matrilineal and patriarchal, and the groom goes to live with the bride's family in a patriarchal culture. Such family systems do exist. Interestingly, it is the wife's brother who tends to be the patriarchal figure in the family. If the couple have children, the uncle is the authoritarian figure for the children.

Next, in a very general way let us look at family systems around the world. When sociologists and other scholars discuss international differences they typically divide the cultures of the world into two general categories: the more developed nations and the less developed nations. With respect to family systems more developed countries are usually defined as having **modern family systems** and less developed countries are said to have **traditional family systems.**

Two points need to be made here before these terms are explained. First, the terms *traditional* and *modern* may evoke certain judgments on the part of the reader. Some think of *modern* as meaning that something is inherently better than something described as *traditional*. Other readers may have the opposite reaction. Neither view is accurate for those wishing to take a scholarly approach. For researchers, *modern* and *traditional* are descriptive terms devoid of notions of better or worse.

The second point prior to explaining these terms is that no society is completely modern or completely traditional. Within traditional societies there will be found families following a modern pattern of family life. Within modern societies, there are certainly traditional families. When these terms are used they describe the modal or most typical pattern one might find in the society being studied.

What are some of the characteristics of a traditional family system? First, family elders may arrange marriages. Historically, in many societies children did not find their own mates. This was done by other family members or by matchmakers. Children oftentimes had the right of refusal—they could say they did not wish to marry the person selected for them—but they were not directly involved in the selection process.

Second, the reasons for marriage were largely practical or economic. Marriages were made to foster alliances among different family groupings or for economic alliances. Love and individual choice did not play a role. Therefore, marital intimacy was not a high priority. As a result, in many marriages husbands and wives may have had little communication and emotional connections to each other.

Third, families had high fertility rates and large numbers of children were born. In part this was due to the fact that large numbers of children also died. Those children who did survive lived a family life that was very much adult-centered. From an early age, children were taught to focus on the well-being of their parents and of the family unit overall. The needs of the family greatly outweighed any individual needs.

Fourth, divorce rates are much lower in traditional societies than in modern societies. (This will be discussed later on in a separate chapter.) For the sake of this chapter, it should be noted that divorce was seen as absolutely inappropriate in a number of traditional societies. If divorce were permitted, it very often was the decision of the husband, with the wife having little or no rights in the matter.

Lastly, the traditional family tended toward the extended type. Although not always the case, traditional families were connected to their extended kin, and to some degree even to the larger community. Both family and community, in traditional societies, defined who individuals were and their place in society.

Modern family systems have characteristics opposite those noted for traditional family systems. First, mate selection is seen as a relatively free process, and individuals have the right to select their own marriage partners without the interference of elders. Second, marriage in modern societies is based on emotional needs. There is a great desire for intimacy, nurturance, and emotional connectedness between marital partners. Third, death rates have dropped precipitously and children have a much greater chance for survival today than in the past. Couples who do have children have fewer children. The children they do have grow up in family environments much different from those of children in the past. Today, families tend to be child-centered: parents focus on the well-being of the children over and above their own needs. Fourth, divorce is much more widespread in modern societies. Either marriage partner has the right to initiate divorce proceedings. In some modern societies it is rare not to find at least one divorce in any given group of adult siblings. Fifth, in modern family systems, there is a tendency toward the nuclear family type. This does not mean that these family units are cut off from extended kin. We know that there continue to be connections between extended kin in modern societies, but, given geographic mobility, these connections may be maintained by the telephone, E-mail, and other modern forms of communication, as opposed to regular face-to-face interaction.

There are two additional points that need to be made regarding the differences between traditional and modern societies. A major underlying value in modern societies is the idea of **efficacy**. *Efficacy* is the belief that one can take control of one's own life. In a way, it is a belief that each of us can influence our own destiny. **Fatalism** is the opposite of efficacy. *Fatalism* is the belief that one does not control one's destiny. Events occur beyond one's control and the individuals have little, if any, control over their own lives. Efficacy tends to be a widespread belief in modern societies, while fatalism is a common belief held by people living in traditional societies.

These beliefs may influence the nature of family life. For example, in modern societies the value of efficacy may affect fertility. In modern societies individuals believe they have the right, and the ability, to make sound judgments about when to have children and how many children to have. Therefore, the use of contraception is supported by the value of efficacy. In traditional societies, where the value of fatalism is present, children are often seen as a "gift from God" and there may be less use of contraceptive technology and fertility rates will be higher than in modern societies.

A second additional point of comparison, and one we will return to throughout the book, is the role of women in society. In traditional societies, gender roles—what it means to be female or male—are clearly defined. Simply put, in traditional societies men are A, B, C and women are D, E, and F. There are dramatic differences in the expected roles and behaviors of men and women. In most instances, this also involves clear-cut power distinctions, with women having characteristics similar to minority groups: less power and less opportunity in the economic and educational spheres of life. In modern society, gender-role differences, although still present, tend not to be so dramatically differentiated. In modern societies, women appear to have greater opportunities across the spectrum of social and economic life.

These two elements, efficacy and fatalism, are related to gender roles. Because fatalistic societies believe that the roles of men and women are predetermined, the opportunities for women, and, in a way for men, are limited. Societies that emphasize the value of efficacy tend to hold that everyone—men and women—can influence his or her own destiny, and can become whatever his or her intelligence, talent, and abilities make possible. In doing the exercises in this chapter, keep in mind these two underlying elements of modern and traditional societies.

The exercises in this chapter will explore some of the international patterns in family life today. Data for both traditional and modern societies are included for analysis. In order to gain some understanding of these international differences, there is data from seven countries: China, France, India, Italy, Malawi, Mexico, and the United States. China and India are the two most populous countries in the world. France and Italy are examples of modern societies. Mexico and Malawi are representative of traditional societies. The United States is included for comparative purposes. All countries will not be represented in every table because data were not available for some topics.

Analysis

TABLE 1.1 *Population, Fifteen Years and over by Marital Status for Selected Countries*

Country (Year)	Total	Single	Married	Widowed	Separated or Divorced
China (1990)	818,357,560	205,652,610	557,747,990	50,123,760	4,833,200
France (1991)	52,333,700	20,517,300	25,755,400	3,950,500	2,110,500
India (1992–93)	NA	NA	NA	NA	NA
Italy (1991)	47,932,979	14,506,776	28,348,522	4,223,775	853,906
Malawi (1992)	NA	NA	NA	NA	NA
Mexico (1990)	45,140,304	16,461,960	25,565,033	2,029,861	1,083,450
United States (1995)	202,727,000	54,977,000	109,887,000	13,365,000	24,498,000

Source: U.S. Census Bureau, *International DataBase.*

TABLE 1.1A *Percentage Distribution of Population by Marital Status for Selected Countries*

Country (Year)	Total	Single	Married	Widowed	Separated or Divorced
China (1990)					
France (1991)					
India (1992–93)		42.7	51.4	5.4	0.5
Italy (1991)					
Malawi (1992)		17.1	68.5	1.7	7.6
Mexico (1990)					
United States (1995)					

Source: U.S. Census Bureau, *International DataBase.*

1. Table 1.1 presents data on marital status. Calculate the percent distribution of the population by marital status and place your answers in Table 1.1A. Raw data were not available for India and Malawi. However, the Census Bureau does provide percent distribution by marital status, and these data are included in Table 1.1A. Note that Malawi's numbers do not add up to 100 percent. Approximately 5.1 percent of Malawi's population lives in consensual unions. The data for Mexico exclude the consensual union and unknown categories as reported by the Census Bureau.

2. What similarities do you find in the data?

3. What differences do you find in the data?

4. How does the United States compare to the other countries listed?

TABLE 1.2   *Age-Specific Fertility Rates (15–19) and Total Fertility Rates by Selected Country, 2001*

Country	Age-Specific Fertility Rate (15–19)	Total Fertility Rate
China	9.0	1.8
France	7.3	1.7
India	53.6	3.0
Italy	6.6	1.2
Malawi	114.6	5.2
Mexico	44.0	2.6
United States	58.5	2.0

Source: U.S. Census Bureau, *International DataBase.*

5. Human reproduction and the socialization of children are a central concern of family life in all cultures. The number of children women have and the ages at which they have them varies from culture to culture. Table 1.2 presents data on **total fertility rates** and **age-specific fertility rates.** Total fertility rates project how many children an entire generation of women will have when they have stopped having children. This is often reported as averages. For example, in China women have a total fertility rate of 1.8, but it is obvious that it is impossible to have 0.8 of a child! What this statistic really means is that, for every 1,000 women of childbearing age, they will end up producing 1,800 children. If you divide 1,800 children by 1,000 women, the average per woman is 1.8. Age-specific fertility rates (ASFR) report the actual number of children born to women in a specific age category per 1,000 women in that age category. Again, as an example we can look at China. Women of fifteen to nineteen years of age have an ASFR of 9.0. In the year 2000 (reported in 2001), for every 1,000 Chinese women aged fifteen to nineteen, there were nine births. Based on the data in the table, how do modern societies compare to the traditional societies with respect to total fertility rates?

6. How do they compare with respect to ASFRs?

7. What factors may contribute to the high rates for Malawi?

8. What factors may help explain the low rates for China, France, and Italy?

TABLE 1.3 *Prevalence of Contraceptive Use among Women Twenty Years and over for Selected Countries and Years*

Country	Year Surveyed	Percentage Range of Use
China	1988	38–91
France	1998	70–87
India	1992–93	21–61
Italy	1979	78–81
Malawi	1996	18–28
Mexico	1987	34–62
United States	1990	60–78

Source: U.S. Census Bureau, *International DataBase.*

9. One factor that may influence fertility is the availability and use of contraception. Table 1.3 presents data on contraception use among women of various age groups. Because of this variability by age, the table indicates the range of use for each country. How would you compare contraceptive use between modern and traditional societies?

10. Why might modern societies have higher rates of usage?

11. Why might traditional societies have lower rates of usage?

12. What general statements can be made about differences in family systems based on an examination of these data?

Selected Bibliography and Suggested Readings _____

Ambert, Anne-Marie. (2001). *Families in the new millennium*. Boston: Allyn & Bacon.

Demo, David. (Ed.). (2001). *Handbook of family diversity*. New York: Oxford University Press.

Goode, William. (1970). *World revolution and family patterns*. New York: Free Press.

Mason, Mary Ann, Skolnick, Arlene, & Sugarman, Stephen. (Eds.). (1998). *All our families: New policies for a new century*. New York: Oxford University Press.

Mindel, Charles, Habenstein, Robert, & Wright, Roosevelt. (Eds.). (1998). *Ethnic families in America: Patterns and variations* (4th ed.). Upper Saddle River, NJ: Prentice-Hall.

Murdock, George. (1949). *Social structure*. New York: Macmillan.

Schneider, Linda, & Silverman, Arnold. (1997). *Global sociology: Introducing five contemporary societies*. Boston: McGraw-Hill.

Weeks, John. (1999). *Population: An introduction to concepts and issues* (7th ed.). Belmont, CA: Wadsworth.

Yorburg, Betty. (2002). *Family realities: A global view*. Upper Saddle River, NJ: Prentice-Hall.

2

Whom Do We Marry?

Marriage and the Norm of Endogamy in the United States

In the United States we like to think that people marry whomever they choose. Americans often make fun of those cultures in which parents or some stranger called a matchmaker select someone's mate. What most students don't realize is that even in the United States mate selection is not a completely "free" process. To some degree, the society or groups of which one is a member influence the selection of husbands and wives.

Sociologists have long maintained that all mate selection is influenced by the larger society. All societies appear to have two **norms** or expectations that influence our decision making with respect to whom we marry. First, there is the **norm of exogamy.** The norm of exogamy may be viewed as a kind of boundary line. Everyone inside the boundary line is prohibited to you as a sexual and marriage partner. You must go outside the boundary line to find a mate. This may be easier to conceptualize if one thinks of the **incest taboo.**

The norm of exogamy works in the same way. As with the incest taboo, certain categories of persons are prohibited as sexual partners. We often think of the incest taboo as including mothers and fathers, brothers and sisters, uncles, aunts, and other members of our extended kin. The incest taboo, however, is quite variable, and its definition varies from culture to culture. Even within the United States, where incest is a crime, states have different legal definitions of what constitutes the crime of incest.

All societies place limitations on whom one may marry. Remember that the norm of exogamy forces one to go outside a boundary line to seek a partner. No society permits persons to go out into infinite space, so to speak, to find a partner. One is not free to select anyone outside his or her family. Sociologists refer to these expectations as the **norm of endogamy.** The norm of endogamy serves as a second boundary line, one that you must remain within. The space between the norm of exogamy and the norm of endogamy defines the area of socially acceptable partners. Anyone who falls between the two boundary lines is a person defined by society as a socially acceptable marriage partner for you.

Different societies define endogamy in different ways. It should be somewhat obvious that who you might deem as a socially acceptable partner depends on what group you belong to and the norm of endogamy for that particular group. In the history of the United States, endogamy has been defined by very specific variables. Let us examine each of these in turn.

The first endogamous variable is **age**. Traditionally, in most societies older men married younger women. The age differences were oftentimes quite large, falling somewhere between ten and fifteen years. This was due largely to economic factors and based on patriarchal norms. Men were the major providers for their wives. They needed some number of years to become economically established. On the other hand, younger women were seen as desirable because of their potential as child bearers. As a result, it was not unusual for a man in his mid-thirties to marry a woman who was still in her teens. Today there appears to be a movement toward **age homogamy**. Husbands and wives are now more similar in ages compared to their historical counterparts. Interestingly, if a much older male marries a younger female now it is seen as an oddity, a reversal of the historical pattern.

Note that in this discussion there is also the issue of gender, whereby husbands are supposed to be older than their wives. While there have always been some exceptions to this norm, today there may be greater numbers of older wives (see Table 2.3). This may be due to the changing ideologies and gender roles pertaining to women, and to an increasing degree of individual choice in marriage.

A second important endogamous variable in the American experience is **race**. This is perhaps the strongest endogamous variable. Historically and overwhelmingly, people married within their own racial categories as custom and law defined these categories.

The root factor for racial endogamy was slavery. The United States instituted a legally enforced system of race slavery. Race defined one's legal status. Therefore, there had to be, in a legal sense, clear definitions of who was black and who was not black. Interracial marriage would confound this definition: how does one label the offspring of a black–white marriage? Many states resolved this issue by outlawing interracial marriages. These state laws remained in force until 1967 when the Supreme Court ruled in *Loving v. Commonwealth of Virginia* (1967) that no state could forbid marriages between two consenting adults on the basis of color. While there are no longer any laws forbidding such marriages, black–white intermarriages are still rare (see Table 2.4).

The same cannot be said for the other major racial category used in the United States. Asian Americans appear to have increasing levels of interracial marriages. This is especially true for Japanese Americans, whose intermarriage rate is approximately 50 percent. This may be explained in part by the relatively high level of education among Japanese Americans, and by the growing acceptance of Japanese Americans as marriage partners by white Americans.

A third important endogamous variable is **social class.** Social class consists of a group of persons who share the same social position in society. Social class is determined largely by wealth, power, and social prestige. Sociologists often use three measures to determine social class: education, occupation, and income. Social class is a powerful endogamous variable. Powerful, in the sense that most people marry others who occupy the same social class. In many ways social class is what sociologists consider to be a **master status.** We may hold many status positions at one time, but a few status positions seem to have overriding importance in terms of how we are viewed by others and how we view ourselves. In the United States, sex, race, and social class are all master statuses. As a master status then, social class has a great deal of influence on us. It may determine what neighborhood we live in, who we interact with, the schools we go to, the people we date, and the person we eventually marry. Our social worlds tend not be random. We socialize in a world defined by social class parameters. This was true in the past and remains true today.

A fourth variable is **religion.** At one time religion was as powerful an endogamous variable as race and social class. People married within their own religious category. Today there appears to be a major shift in this pattern. It is difficult to measure the actual number of interreligious marriages, however, because the Census Bureau does not ask information regarding one's religious background. Information is gathered by examining a variety of smaller surveys.

There is growing evidence that interreligious marriages are increasing. Some estimates suggest that between one quarter and one third of all Catholics and Protestants marry outside their religion. Jewish Americans appear to have the highest rate of outmarriage with some estimates suggesting that the rate is now over 50 percent. (Reasons for these changes in interreligious marriages will be discussed later.)

A last variable to be discussed is **ethnic group affiliation.** As a result of the immigration process a number of distinct ethnic–immigrant communities were formed in the United States. Historically, these ethnic groups were very endogamous. Most Irish Americans married other Irish Americans, most Italian Americans married Italian Americans, and so on. Today there is a substantial degree of interethnic marriage, especially among the older immigrant groups. For newer arrivals, endogamy may still be the norm. However, as assimilation processes proceed one may project similar patterns of intermarriage for these newer groups as they move through the generations.

These are the usual definitions of endogamy in the United States. Understand that endogamy appears to be a universal norm in that it exists in all cultures. However, there may be some similarities and also some differences in how endogamy is defined elsewhere. Having examined how endogamy is defined, I will discuss how we come to learn the norm of endogamy.

Each of you reading this probably has some awareness as to the type of person you are supposed to marry. That is, there are certain categories of people of whom, if you brought them home and introduced one of them as your betrothed your parents, extended kin, and friends would disapprove. How did you learn who was acceptable and who was not? This information might have been communicated directly or indirectly. Obviously, when a parent makes a statement like, "If you bring *one of them* home I'll kill myself," it conveys an explicit piece of information. Of course, who one of "them" is depends on the group of which you are a member. It also depends on the level of prejudice you are exposed to by your family members.

Most information involving endogamy is indirect information. How is it transmitted? In most cases the process may be very subtle. Who are the marriage partners of other relatives? What is the makeup of marriages we see on television or in the movies? What types of subtle cues are we given by our parents? What is the nature of conversation about "others" we are exposed to in our homes, in our neighborhoods, and in the larger social world? All of these influences may lead us to make certain choices in our dating partners and, eventually, in our marriage partners. These influences may be so subtle that we are not even aware of them. Their effect is cumulative, and may be quite powerful.

In addition to these influences, there are the values and perceptions of the larger culture. How beauty is defined in the culture can certainly influence our perceptions of potential mates. What is seen as attractive in a particular culture? Should the person be tall or short, thin or stocky? Should the women have large breasts or small breasts? Does the amount of wealth the man has matter? Does the amount of wealth the woman has matter? While we often think of attraction as a matter of personal choice, social factors are very important in influencing our individual judgments.

So far we have looked at how endogamy is defined, and how the norm of endogamy is communicated from one generation to the next. The question remains, why do societies have the norm of endogamy? There is a general axiom in sociology that all societies seek to maintain a sense of social order. Social order is typically maintained through the social class system. This, in turn, is maintained through the continuation of the social class system from generation to generation, and this is maintained through the system of endogamous marriages. If A marries C, instead of marrying B, that challenges the existing social order because how the offspring of the marriage will be positioned in the social class system is ambiguous.

As an example, consider the subject of race. Remember that black–white marriages were not permitted in a number of states in the United States prior to 1967 due to the legacy of slavery. Why was this the case? In the southern slave system no whites were slaves. Slavery was solely based on race. If you were black, with some exceptions, you were a slave. What, then, happens if a white marries a black? What is the status of the child? These mixed offspring would certainly raise questions about the entire system of slavery. In order to avoid this conundrum, these kinds of unions were outlawed. As for illicit relationships between blacks and whites, in most cases white males and black females, the offspring were given the status of their mothers. They were slaves.

Let us take this analysis one step further. If everyone learned the norm of endogamy, why the need to pass laws against interracial marriages? The answer to this question, simply put, is love. Love is an interesting emotion. Almost every popular song ever produced speaks to love. Think of the number of poems, novels, movies, and plays that deal with love.

Love, however, is also interesting from a sociological point of view. Love has two characteristics that make it important. First, love seems to be unpredictable. It appears to have the potential to develop between any two persons at any given time. Even people who are not supposed to fall in love, in terms of the society's norms, may fall in love. As noted above, this unpredictability is not acceptable in a society concerned with maintaining social order.

A second characteristic of love that may challenge society's sense of order is its intensity. People tend not to fall in love a "little bit." We often think of love as an all-or-nothing emotion. Love can be very intense. It alters our behavior. It may alter the way we look at others, and even how we look at ourselves. When one is in love one generally feels better about everything. This release of a seemingly uncontrollable emotion may be viewed as very dangerous to society. It may lead people to do things they would not typically do. They may even challenge the norms of the society. Therefore, both the unpredictability and the intensity of love need to be controlled. Thus, the norm of endogamy comes into play.

What of the norm of endogamy today? From the discussion above it becomes apparent that the norm of endogamy is not as strong as it once was. A number of the variables that influence endogamy—race, religion, ethnic group affiliation—all appear to be weakening. More and more individuals appear to be crossing this traditional boundary line to seek marriage partners.

Why is this the case? Several factors may be contributing to this pattern. I can address two of the factors here. First, the influence of religion on everyday life appears to be waning. It is not the case that Americans are not religious. Most Americans, for example, express a belief in the existence of God. However, with respect to their day-to-day lives religion does not exert the influence it may have in the past. This is referred to as the process of **secularization.** With respect to marriage, in the past marriage was seen as a religious contract, very much influenced by the community one lived in. Today, while many couples do have a religious ceremony, and do invite members of their family and social community to the ceremony, they do not necessarily view their marriage as a sacred and communal contract. It is viewed more as an individual contract entered into voluntarily. This sense of individuality leads to the notion that the individual is the one who has the choice of whom to marry, regardless of endogamous influences.

Another factor contributing to changing marriage patterns is the increase in educational attainment. There are now increasing numbers of young men and women who go on to college compared to the past. How does this influence marriage patterns? There are two major impacts on marriage. First, as more and more young people go to college, there are greater opportunities to meet others from diverse backgrounds. The person sitting next to you in class will probably come from a different neighborhood, city, state, or even from a different country. In college, students are exposed to a variety of persons. College, therefore, provides the opportunity to meet people who do not belong to your group.

Second, college also influences how we look at other people. College education is often seen as a liberalizing experience: liberalizing, not necessarily in the sense of political ideology, but in the sense of increasing one's openness to others. The college experience, ideally, exposes students to a variety of ideas, cultures, traditions, and people, combining both opportunity and outlook that may later influence our decision about whom to marry.

In the analysis section of this chapter, you will have the opportunity to examine the norm of endogamy with respect to age and race differences. You will also have the opportunity to analyze the change in marriage rates, and the age at which people marry.

Analysis

TABLE 2.1 *Marital Status by Year (in percentages): 1980–2000*

Marital Status	1980	1990	2000
Never Married	20.3	22.2	27.1
Married	65.5	61.9	56.6
Widowed	10.9	11.7	6.6
Divorced	6.2	8.3	9.7

Source: U.S. Census Bureau, *Statistical Abstract of the United States: 2000,* Table 53; and DP-2. *Profiles of Selected Social Characteristics: 2000.*

1. Table 2.1 presents data on marital status over time. What changes have occurred over the last twenty years?

2. Which marital status category has had the largest change?

3. Why do you believe this is the case?

TABLE 2.2   *Estimated Median Age at First Marriage, by Sex: 1940–2000*

Year	Male	Female
2000	26.8	25.1
1990	26.1	23.9
1980	24.7	22.0
1970	23.2	20.8
1960	22.8	20.3
1950	22.8	20.3
1940	24.3	21.5

Source: U.S. Census Bureau, *Current Population Reports,* p. 20, No. 514, March 1998 (Update), earlier reports, and www.census.gov/population/socdemo/hh-fam/tabms-2.txt

4. The Bureau of the Census has maintained estimates of median ages at first marriage since 1890. The "median" is the midpoint in a series of numbers. For example, as shown in Table 2.2, the median age for first marriage for men in 2000 was 26.8. This means that, for all men who entered first marriages, 50 percent were over 26.8 years, and 50 percent were younger than 26.8 years. Examine the data in the table. For the years 1950 to 1970 women's median age for marriages was twenty. What can we infer from these data about teenage marriages?

5. Which time period indicates the greatest increase in median age of marriage for women?

6. Why do you believe this period showed the greatest increase in median age?

TABLE 2.3 *Married Couples by Differences in Ages between Husband and Wife (in thousands): 1999*

Age Difference	Number	Percent
Total	55,849	
Husband 10 or more years older than wife	4,012	
Husband 6 to 9 years older	6,891	
Husband 5 years or less older	38,103	
Wife 10 or more years older than husband	679	
Wife 6 to 9 years older	1,222	
Wife 5 years or less older	4,942	

Source: U.S. Census Bureau, *Statistical Abstract of the United States: 2000,* Table 56.

7. In addition to the age at which people marry, age differences between brides and grooms is also of interest. Table 2.3 presents data on age differences between husbands and wives. Calculate the percent distribution by age difference category and put your answers in the table.

8. Who is older, husbands or wives?

9. Why do you believe this pattern emerges from the data?

10. Regardless of who is older, what general observations can you make about age differences?

TABLE 2.4   *Interracial Married Couples by Types of Intermarriages (in thousands): 1960–2000*

Year	Total Married Couples	Black/White	White/Other	Black/Other
2000	56,497	363	1,051	50
1990	53,256	211	720	33
1980	49,514	121	785	47
1970	44,598	65	233	12
1960	40,491	51	90	7

Source: U.S. Census Bureau, *Interracial Married Couples: 1960 to Present.* Internet release date: January 7, 1999 and *Interracial Married Couples: 1980 to Present.* Internet release date: February 4, 2002 at www.census.gov/population/socdemo/ms-la/tabms-3.txt; and www.census.gov/population/socdemo/hh-fam/tabms-3.txt

TABLE 2.4A   *Percent Interracial Married Couples by Types of Intermarriages: 1960–1998*

Year	Total Married Couples	Black/White	White/Other	Black/Other
2000				
1990				
1980				
1970				
1960				

Source: U.S. Census Bureau, *Interracial Married Couples: 1960 to Present.* Internet release date: January 7, 1999 at www.census.gov/population/socdemo/ms-la/tabms-3.txt

11. Table 2.4 presents data on interracial marriages. Examine the data in the table and calculate the percent distribution of marriages for each of the categories shown and place the percents in Table 2.4A.

12. What pattern emerges for black–white marriages?

13. White–other marriages?

14. Black–other marriages?

15. Another way to analyze these data is to look at percentage change over time. We can do this by looking at the growth rates of different categories of marriage. This involves a simple computation:

$$\frac{(2000) - 1960}{1960} \times 100 = \text{Percent Change 1960 to 2000}$$

a. Calculate the percent change for total married couples: _____

b. black–white marriages: _____

c. white–other marriages: _____

d. black–other marriages: _____

16. Which category increased at the greatest rate and why do you believe this has occurred?

17. Based on the data you have just analyzed, what general observations can you make about marriage in U.S. society today?

Selected Bibliography and Suggested Readings _____

Bailey, Beth. (1988). *From the front porch to the back seat.* Baltimore: Johns Hopkins University Press.

Barron, Milton. (Ed.). (1972). *The blending of America: Patterns of intermarriage.* Chicago: Quadrangle.

Gordon, Albert. (1964). *Intermarriage.* Boston: Beacon Press.

Laner, Mary. (1995). *Dating: Delights, discontents, and dilemmas* (2nd ed.). Salem, WI: Sheffield.

Murstein, Bernard. (1986). *Paths to marriage.* Beverly Hills: Sage.

Nock, S. L. (1998). *Marriage in men's lives.* New York: Oxford University Press.

Spickard, Paul. (1989). *Mixed blood: Intermarriage and ethnic identity in twentieth-century America.* Madison: University of Wisconsin Press.

Waite, L., & Gallagher, M. (2000). *The case for marriage.* Cambridge, MA: Harvard University Press.

Whyte, M. K. (Ed.). (2000). *Marriage in America: A communitarian perspective.* Lanham, MD: Rowman & Littlefield.

3

Be Fruitful and Multiply: American Fertility Patterns

In most definitions of the family children hold a central place. Human offspring are dependent on adults for survival for a much longer time than offspring of other species. Baby birds can take flight and survive in a relatively short time after their birth. Babies cannot survive in the nonhuman environment until after a long period of socialization. The family may very well have developed because of this need for long-term support of offspring. As a result, in many cultures, the major reason for marriage is procreation. In the sociology of the family, two terms emerged that indicate the central position of children in our thinking about the family. Sociologists speak of the **family of orientation**, the family in which we are raised. In our family of orientation we are the children. Many adults also form a **family of procreation** in which they raise children as parents. In both cases, many people see themselves in relation to children.

In order to get some sense of childbearing patterns, we turn to the field of **demography**. *Demography* is the scientific study of population. **Demographers** are professionals who study population patterns and trends. Demographers study three components of population as well: **fertility, mortality,** and **migration.** Migration is the movement of persons from one place to another. Mortality includes death rates and causes of death. Fertility is the study of births and birth rates, the focus of this chapter.

Fertility varies from culture to culture. Even within cultures, fertility can vary from group to group. What are some of the factors that influence fertility? In almost every culture, it is the less educated who are likely to have higher fertility rates. At the same time, in many cultures the highest educated groups may have the lowest fertility rates. This especially holds true if one looks at the educational status of women. Higher educated women are more likely to have a broader range of career opportunities. Concern with career development, in turn, may limit the number of children born to any given woman. Both education and work patterns thus influence the fertility of women in every society.

The availability and use of contraception may influence fertility. Note that there are two elements important for contraception to play a role in society. First, the contraception technology must be available. From a sociological perspective, however, it is the second factor that is the more interesting. Even if the technology is available it does not mean that it will be utilized. What also must be present for its use is a value system whereby people feel comfortable using the technology. Comfort here does not refer to physical comfort, although that too may be a factor. Rather, comfort here means emotional comfort. Is there a religious precept that condemns the use of contraception? Is there a strong cultural or economic motivation to have children? If these elements are present, then, even if contraception is available, it may not be widely used.

Fertility may also be influenced by social values. Throughout most of U.S. history, with the exception of the post–World War II era, there has been a gradual and continuing decline in fertility. During the 1950s, and lasting into the early 1960s, the United States experienced what has since been called "the baby boom." What this boom involved was large numbers of women having third and fourth children. Births averaged over 4,000,000 per year, the highest it had ever been up to that point in U.S. history.

What accounted for this sudden increase in births? There were a number of factors that contributed to this reversal of the historical pattern of lower fertility. First, post-war periods often find increases in fertility, because large numbers of men return from war, marry, and have children. Second, during the 1950s there was one of the largest expansions in the U.S. economy. With the shift from industrial to a postindustrial society, larger numbers of people began to enter white-collar middle-class occupations. More people were now making more money, and more of them could afford to have third and fourth children. A third factor had to do with the perceived role of women. During World War II a number of women worked in a variety of fields because large numbers of men were off fighting in the war. After the war, the men returned, and the women were expelled from the workforce. While poorer and immigrant women always worked, men thought the place of their middle-class counterparts belonged in the home. Their major roles were limited to wife, mother, and homemaker. In a society where these roles were the major roles for women, it is not surprising that fertility would increase.

Since the early 1960s, there has been a decline in fertility. What has accounted for this decline? The major factor appears to be the changing role of women in society. Larger numbers of young women are attending college. There has been a dramatic influx of women into the workforce, even in what had been traditional male occupations like accounting and law. For more and more women, the role of mother is no longer the only role they strive to achieve. There are growing opportunities for success and a sense of personal worth available to women today, and these other options appear to have a substantial impact on fertility.

Also, there has been a shift in values regarding fertility. During the 1950s, if a woman had two children, a common question was, when are you going to have your third? Today, if a woman has two children and is pregnant with her third, her friends might ask her why she is having a third. This example illustrates an attitudinal shift. Social pressure is again at play here but it reverses traditional patterns. Instead of the pressure being **pronatal**, desiring many children, it is now **antinatal**, the desire to limit fertility. In part this shift may be explained by the notion of **quality over quantity.** Today more and more adults seem to have the number of children to whom they can offer maximum benefits. For example, if adults feel it is important for their children to attend college, they may wonder how many children they can have and still afford to send them all to college. This desire to maximize the experiences of their children may play a major role in limiting current fertility.

While the average number of children women have has declined, people still have children. Let us look next at some of the motivations to have children. Certainly one of the most important is the social pressure to have children. Almost all societies value children. In many cultures having a child is the true identifier of adulthood. In many instances one's own parents may not recognize their children as adults until their children produce grandchildren.

Social pressure is also something that lies outside the family. Let us return to the 1950s for a moment. Remember that large numbers of women were having third and fourth children during this period. Now let us say you live in just such a community. You have two children. You begin to see that all your friends and neighbors are having third and/or fourth children. While you may not think this would have any effect on your fertility decisions, sociologists suggest that it might. We are all social beings, and our social environment can influence us. Certainly not everyone would be so influenced, but it is equally unlikely that no one would be influenced by the behavior of others.

In addition to these external pressures, there are certainly individual motivations to have children. A widespread motivation is the desire to pass on the family name. Having children may be part and parcel of family tradition. It offers people the opportunity to develop a sense of continuity. Their parents represent the past, they represent the present, and their children represent the future. In some sense, having children may give people a sense of immortality.

Children also give people an opportunity to expand their own selves. The concept of self is what sociologists use to refer to the composite identities we develop for ourselves. In some respects, it is similar to the psychological term *personality*. Having children means we become mothers or fathers, and the actual playing of these roles expands our sense of self. We need to call on practical and emotional resources we would not use if we were not parents. Becoming a parent allows us to take a new look at ourselves, and also, perhaps, to look at the world in new and unique ways.

In many cultures there are economic motivations to have children. This is especially true in agricultural societies where children are seen as economic assets because they can help with the labor-intensive activities of farm life. In many countries children are also seen as one's social security system, as caretakers for their elders. Boys are desired over girls because of their ability to do hard labor. Girls can do hard labor as well but they are often not recognized as equal to boys. Girls may have economic worth as well because, when they are of marriageable age, they may fetch a **bride price**, money or economic resources that will have to be paid to the parent of the bride.

In industrial societies there appears to be little economic motivation to have children. In fact, the reverse appears to be true. In industrialized societies children are often seen as economic liabilities. It costs a great deal of money to raise them, including expenses from diapers to the cost of a college education, and then, just when they can earn their own keep, they pick up, leave home, and set up their own households.

A motivation to have children that is sometimes mentioned by people is to help their marriage. The belief is that children will bring a couple together. The truth, in fact, may be counterintuitive. Children are not therapists. They do not counsel adults nor do they bring the couple closer. Children do not resolve marital problems. Research indicates that children can exacerbate an already troubled marriage because they are totally dependent upon their parents. They need physical care and emotional support. A couple going through marital difficulties will not have their problems solved by a nine-month-old infant or, for that matter, by a fourteen-year-old adolescent.

Having a child may also make one feel "grown-up." One might think that this should work the other way around. One perhaps should feel grown up prior to having a child. This may be a factor in the widely debated issue of teenage parenthood. The actual number of births to teenagers has steadily declined, not increased, as many people believe (see Table 3.4). What has changed is the marital status of the mothers. In the past many teenage mothers were married, either prior to or after conception. Today many of those teenagers who do become mothers do not marry, at least during the pregnancy. What motivates these women to have children? There is no clear-cut or universal answer to this question. One possible explanation may be the desire to feel grown up. Another may be the lack of understanding and/or the lack of use of contraception. Yet another factor may be social pressure. In certain areas, it may be the case that the young woman's girlfriends are also having children out of wedlock. Therefore, having a child is part of the normative behavior for the group. This issue has entered the world of politics. Elected officials are debating whether or not federal monies should be spent developing policies that would encourage marriage.

In this chapter you will have the opportunity to examine contemporary fertility rates, fertility rates over time, fertility by age, and also by marital status.

Analysis

TABLE 3.1 *Live Births (in thousands) and Total Fertility Rates: 1960 to 1999*

Year	Births	Total Fertility Rate
1960	4,258	3,449
1970	3,731	2,094
1980	3,612	1,840
1990	4,158	2,081
1999	3,958	

Source: U.S. Census Bureau, *Statistical Abstract of the United States: 2000,* Tables 77, 82; U.S. National Center for Health Statistics, *National Vital Statistics Report,* 48, 14, (August 8, 2000).

TABLE 3.2 *Age-Specific Fertility Rates (ASFR) in the United States: 1999*

Age of Mother	ASFR	ASFR × 5
15–19	49.6	
20–24	111.0	
25–29	117.8	
30–34	89.6	
35–39	38.3	
40–44	7.4	
Total Fertility Rate		

Source: U.S. National Center for Health Statistics, *National Vital Statistics Report,* 48, 14 (August 8, 2000).

1. Table 3.1 presents data on total number of live births and on total fertility rates. The live births represent the actual number of babies born in the given year. Total fertility rates are the expected total number of lifetime births for every 1,000 women in their childbearing years. The total fertility rate for 1999 was not available when these data were gathered, so you will have to calculate it. This involves a relatively simple calculation. In order to do the calculation you need to know the age-specific fertility rates (ASFR) for each age category for childbearing women (15–44). Once you know the ASFR all you have to do is multiply the ASFR by 5, then add all the sums. The result is the total fertility rate. Complete Table 3.2, and find the total fertility rate for 1999. Remember to place your result in the appropriate space in Table 3.1.

2. How would you describe the general pattern for births and total fertility rates?

3. Which decade experienced the greatest decline?

4. Why do you believe this occurred during this time period?

TABLE 3.3 *Age-Specific Fertility Rates: 1950 to 1999*

Age of Mother	1999	1970	1950	Percent Change 1950–1999
15–19	49.6	68.3	81.6	
20–24	111.0	167.8	196.6	
25–29	117.8	145.1	166.1	
30–34	89.6	73.3	103.7	
35–39	38.3	31.7	52.9	
40–44	7.4	8.1	15.1	

Source: U.S. National Center for Health Statistics, *National Vital Statistics Report,* 48, 3 and 14 (2000).

5. Age-Specific Fertility Rates may be compared over time. This allows us to determine whether women's childbearing patterns are changing. Examine the data in Table 3.3. In the appropriate space calculate the percent change in ASFRs between 1950 and 1999.

$$\text{Percent Change} = \frac{1999 - 1950}{1950} \times 100$$

6. Which age category experienced the greatest decline in rate of births per 1,000 women?

7. Why do you believe this category had the greatest decline?

8. Which age category had the greatest percent decline?

9. Why is this the case?

10. What overall pattern did you find?

11. What factors influenced the overall pattern you find in Table 3.3?

TABLE 3.4 *Birth Rates of Teens (per thousand) by Age Category: 1960 to 1999*

Year	10–14 Years	15–17 Years	18–19 Years
1960	0.8	43.9	166.7
1970	1.2	38.8	114.7
1980	1.1	32.5	82.1
1990	1.4	37.5	88.6
1999	0.9	28.7	80.2

Source: U.S. National Center for Health Statistics, *National Vital Statistics Report,* 48, 3 and 14 (2000).

12. One major issue often discussed related to fertility is teenage pregnancy. Table 3.4 presents data on teenage fertility (actual births, not pregnancies) for various age subgroups. What overall trend do you find after examining these data?

13. Which age category has the highest birth rates?

14. Why do you believe this is the case?

15. What is the rate for the very young teenagers?

16. Why do you believe the topic of teenage pregnancy has become a major issue in society?

TABLE 3.5   *Fertility Indicators, Women 40–44 Years Old (in percentages): June 1976 and June 2000*

	1976	2000
All Women: Children Born	3,091 per 1,000	1,913 per 1,000
None	10.2	19.0
One	9.6	16.4
Two	21.7	35.0
Three	22.7	19.1
Four or more	35.9	10.5
Never-Married Women	724 per 1,000	920 per 1,000
None	75.5	59.6
One	8.7	14.4
Two or more	15.8	25.9

Source: U.S. Census Bureau, *Fertility of American Women: June 1998* (September 2000), pp. 20–526; and *Fertility of American Women: June 2000,* Issued October 2001 (P20-543RV).

17. One reason you may have included in your answer to question 14 was the issue of out-of-wedlock births. Table 3.5 presents data on this topic. Let us examine some of these data. Which categories experienced increases during the time period noted?

18. Which categories experienced declines?

19. How might you compare the "all women" category with the "never-married" category?

20. From the data, what general direction is fertility taking in the United States today, and what may be the implications of this pattern for the future of the family?

Selected Bibliography and Suggested Readings _____

Ambert, Anne-Marie. (1997). *Parents, children and adolescents: Interactive relationships and development in context.* New York: Haworth.

Aries, P. (1962). *Centuries of childhood: A social history of family life.* New York: Vintage.

Cowan, C., & Cowan, P. (2000). *When partners become parents: The big life change for couples.* Mahwah, NJ: Erlbaum.

Glassner, Barry. (1999). *The culture of fear.* New York: Basic Books.

Hamner, T., & Turner, P. (2001). *Parenting in contemporary society* (4th ed.). Boston: Allyn & Bacon.

Hays, Sharon. (1996). *The cultural contradictions of motherhood.* New Haven: Yale University Press.

Kaplan, E. B. (1997). *Not our kind of girl: Unraveling the myths of black teenage motherhood.* Berkeley: University of California Press.

Light, Paul. (1988). *Baby boomers.* New York: W. W. Norton.

Logan, J. R., & Spitze, G. (1996). *Family ties: Enduring relations between parents and their grown children.* Philadelphia: Temple University Press.

Lupton, D., & Barclay, L. (1997). *Constructing fatherhood: Discourses and experiences.* Thousand Oaks, CA: Sage.

Sharp, S. (2000). *The ways we love.* New York: Guilford.

Walzer, S. (1998). *Thinking about the baby: Gender and transitions into parenthood.* Philadelphia: Temple University Press.

Weeks, John. (1999). *Population: An introduction to concepts and issues* (7th ed.). Belmont, CA: Wadsworth.

Children in America: Child-Centered or Child-Forgotten?

The previous chapter examined issues related to the decision whether or not to have children. What happens once children are born? Children are born into a specific family. At the same time they are born into a particular culture. Both family and culture will influence their **socialization process.** In common parlance, the socialization process is referred to as the growing-up process. In sociological terms, it is the process by which a child internalizes the values and norms of the society.

It is certainly true that one's parents and extended kin influence who we are and who we become. The personalities of our parents, their values, beliefs, and parenting style create a social and emotional environment that serves as a model for our own behavior. Children are not pieces of clay to be molded by others. Each of us is born with certain predispositions to develop in a particular manner. Each of us is also an active participant in our own socialization. Unlike other species, humans do not live by instincts. We have the unique ability to interact with our environment.

More specifically, when we think of instincts we can imagine that, if a certain stimulus (**S**) is given to all members of a species, they will respond (**R**) in the same way. Humans, however, are somewhat different. When given a stimulus, humans interpret (**I**) the stimulus and then respond. Schematically, we can show this difference in the following way:

Animals   **S-R**
Humans   **S-I-R**

That *I* is very significant. How do we come to interpret stimuli in different ways? In all likelihood, it is a combination of our specific genetic characteristics and the social and environmental factors of our upbringing. For example, let us take the interaction of a parent and a child. While oftentimes children are very much like their parents, they are not carbon copies of their parents. That is, children are both similar to and different from their parents. Parents expose their children to a variety of ideas, norms, values, and so on. Children interpret these. They come to accept some of the values, and reject others, or they may shape these values in a manner of their own making.

Another example of the interpretive quality of socialization would be to examine the differences between siblings. Do a thought experiment. Think of any group of siblings you may know. They may be your own brothers and/or sisters or other sibling pairs with which you are familiar. Think about their similarities and differences. Often you may be struck by the degree of difference that exists between siblings.

Why is this the case? Didn't they have the same set of parents? In actuality, there are many reasons why siblings are different. First, each child has her/his own unique set of genetic components, so even at birth there are differences. Second, research indicates that birth order affects our socialization. Older children tend to have characteristics that differ from those of their younger siblings. Obviously, the oldest child in the family, at least for some period of time, was an only child. The second child will interact with her/his parents and the sibling. Interaction patterns within families are altered successively with the birth of each child.

A final factor that may influence differences among siblings is the fact that, in a sense, each child has a different set of parents. This may sound like nonsense, but let me explain. Parents do not remain the same throughout their lives. They age, and they change. While we often think of parents socializing children, children also socialize parents. As with all of us, each new experience changes the perception and attitudes of the parents. This will certainly influence their feelings and the manner in which they behave. Children make that kind of impact on their parents. Therefore, to some degree, each child in the same family has a different set of parents. (The reader may realize that this discussion has omitted a very important variable related to childhood socialization—the sex of the child. The sex of the child is such an important variable that the next chapter [Chapter 5] will focus on this one characteristic.)

One major way in which parents influence children is the **parenting style** they use. Historically, there appear to be three main parenting styles. Perhaps the oldest parenting style is the **authoritarian approach**, which emphasizes the importance of obedience. Children are taught to obey the parents. Physical forms of punishment are utilized in this approach, and the parents are often seen as stern taskmasters. This approach may be viewed as parent-centered. The major criticism of this approach is that children are not taught to think for themselves, and will tend to think in extremes: something is either all good or all bad.

The **permissive approach** developed in the early part of the twentieth century and was influenced by the work of Sigmund Freud and others. This approach may be viewed as child-centered. Children were permitted to develop in their own way and given a great deal of freedom. It was felt that any frustration the child might experience would lead to emotional difficulties later on in life. The major criticism of this approach is that children become very egocentric and not understand that they must live in the world with others. The children would not learn that self-interest sometimes has to take second place to the needs of others.

The **authoritative approach** to parenting is a third parenting style. This approach combines elements of the first two approaches. It asserts that children should be allowed to develop in their own unique manner; however, they must also come to realize that they are not alone in the world. Children need to learn that their lives are entwined with the lives of others.

Parenting styles present a good example of how individual behavior is related to the larger culture. Each of these parenting styles emerges in particular types of cultures. The authoritative approach is more common in less industrialized, more traditional, agricultural societies. In these **agrarian societies**, the labor of the children is essential for the economic well-being of the family. Children need to learn to obey the demands of their parents because the cows must be milked, the wheat must be harvested, and so on. Such societies also tend to have larger families, and we find the authoritarian approach more often in societies with high fertility rates. In order to maintain stability within the family and a sense of order in the larger community, individuality is curtailed and group consensus is emphasized.

As stated earlier, the permissive approach emerged in the early part of the twentieth century. This period saw the development and emergence of **industrial societies.** As a result, a number of people were able to move into what we would today call the middle class. Here, the labor of children was not essential to the economic well-being of the family, and it was more beneficial for children to go to school, develop careers, and become economically independent. This better met the demands of an industrial–capitalist society. Children had to learn to fend for themselves. The permissive approach allowed them to explore their own potentialities and find their own place in the urban–industrial system.

The development of the authoritative approach was a reaction to what was seen as the excesses of the first two approaches. If you will, a "middle ground" was seen as necessary with the emergence of postindustrial society. It became more desirable for children to develop a combination of individuality and social conscience. In the modern world, these elements were seen as better suited for both individual good and the collective good.

All three approaches are **ideal types.** Ideal types are theoretical models that allow researchers to compare their theories to reality. In any given society all three types of parenting styles may exist. Sociologists speak of **modal categories,** patterns that appear to be the most common or most desired in any culture at any given time. That is how these parenting styles should be interpreted.

Regardless of the specific parenting style, all children need to develop certain attributes in order to achieve sound and healthy growth. The first of these is to develop a sense of their own emotional well-being. This is, perhaps, the most difficult attribute to measure or discuss. What constitutes good emotional well-being is subject to debate. There is general consensus that all people need a positive sense of self. This does not mean that we need to become egomaniacs; rather, we need to develop a positive self-identity. There is no formula we can follow to achieve this end. Again, the consensus view is that children need a warm, loving environment within which to grow. There may be a variety of ways such an environment can be created.

The second attribute needed for sound development is to help the child develop good intellectual skills. Both sociologists and psychologists have debated the nature of intellectual ability. This debate involves the **nature–nurture controversy.** Some people hold the view that intellectual ability is inborn and genetic (**nature**). Others argue that intellectual ability is a product of the environment in which one is brought up (**nurture**). There is a middle ground to this debate. Many analysts believe that intellectual ability is a product of the interaction of genetics and environment. All children, barring those who have physiological problems, are born with the capacity to learn. Most newborns have a similar range of potentialities, certainly with some degree of variation within that range. What is actually learned is a result of the opportunities presented to the child in her or his social environment.

In order for children to maximize their potential, then, they should be exposed to a variety of stimuli, things like having a variety of colorful and stimulating toys and exposing the child to enriched language such as speaking to the child in complete sentences as opposed to simple phrases. Research also indicates that ongoing interaction is important for intellectual development. The everyday kind of play adults have with children is also important. One should also never underestimate the importance of reading. Reading to even very young children can have a substantial impact on the child. If a loved one reads to the child, the child may come to associate reading with warm feelings and develop a positive attitude toward books. Reading is extremely important to intellectual development throughout one's life.

The third area of development required to achieve healthy adulthood is the ability to interact with others. We live in a social world. A major component of the human experience is learning to live with others. All children need to develop social skills. Throughout their lives, they will interact with a variety of people and find themselves in a variety of social situations. Research indicates the importance of peer relations. Friends and friendships are important, not just for our own pleasure and enjoyment, but also for our own development. Our own sense of self-worth is related to others' perceptions of us. People need to cultivate peer relationships to find validation for their own sense of self.

How do children learn to develop these social skills? Again, some children seem to be "naturally" more social than others. Perhaps there is some inborn, genetic code for sociability. It is more likely that we learn social skills from the social environment. How the people around us interact with each other probably plays a major role in influencing our own social skills. How do one's parents interact with each other? How do our parents interact with others? What are the social norms of sociability in the general culture?

This brief outline indicates some of the outcomes of the socialization process. The process ideally results in children with a healthy emotional repertoire and intellectual and social skills. For sociologists, the larger question is: How does the society help or hinder the process of positive socialization?

From a historical perspective, there is little doubt that the lives of children are better today than in the past. For example, there are much lower rates of infant mortality. Largely due to advances in medical technology and general health care, children have a much better chance of surviving to adulthood. While the quality of education has been widely debated, more children today achieve higher levels of education than ever before in our history. Most children in the United States do not live in poverty, and many children grow up in middle-class homes that have access to a wide variety of material benefits.

On the other hand, the world children grow up in has become more complex and more troubling. Children are confronted with issues of sexuality, drug use, and a variety of situations in which they need to make sound decisions. In the nineteenth century, a child's life may have been laid out for her or him almost from the moment of birth. The child of a carpenter would probably become a carpenter. Today, there are many more choices, and with these choices the dilemma of making good choices. Having choices certainly can be viewed as a good thing. The dilemma is having to decide what choices to make. Most of us, I think, would prefer to have this dilemma than having to live in the world of the nineteenth century.

Unfortunately, not all children appear to have the same options. Some children may still be living in the world of the nineteenth century. As a society, are some children left out? Can we think of our society as child-centered or child-forgotten? Do the policies and programs of our society allow all children the same opportunities to have a positive socialization experience? The analysis section of this chapter will allow you to explore the question through an examination of economic data. Poverty, access to food, child-support payments, and health insurance coverage will each be analyzed.

Analysis

TABLE 4.1 *Persons below Poverty Level by Race and Hispanic Origin, All Persons and Children under 18 Years Old (in percentages): 1970–2001*

Year	All Persons			Children		
	White	Black	Hispanic	White	Black	Hispanic
1970	9.9	33.3	NA	10.5	41.5	NA
1980	10.2	32.5	25.7	13.4	42.1	33.0
1990	10.7	31.9	28.1	15.1	44.2	37.7
2001	9.9	22.7	21.4	13.4	30.2	28.0

Source: U.S. Census Bureau, *Statistical Abstract of the United States: 2000,* Tables 754 and 755; Poverty 1999, March 1999, 2000, and 2001 Current Population Surveys. www.census.gov/hhes/poverty/poverty99/pv99est1.html

1. Poverty has devastating effects on any person who experiences it. This may be especially true for children. Table 4.1 presents data on poverty for all persons and for children under eighteen years old. What general pattern do you find for all people living under the poverty level for the time period covered?

2. What pattern do you find for the children?

3. What comparisons can you draw from the data in comparing poverty rates for all persons and for children?

4. Why do you believe children have higher rates of poverty than do all persons?

TABLE 4.2   *Households and Persons Having Problems with Access to Food (in thousands): 1995 to 1998*

Year	Adults			Children		
	Total Adults	Number	Percentage	Total Children	Number	Percentage
1995	191,063	6,589		70,279	4,100	
1998	197,423	6,135		71,463	3,259	

Source: U.S. Census Bureau, *Statistical Abstract of the United States: 2000,* Table 233.

5. One basic issue facing children in poverty may be having enough food to eat. Table 4.2 examines this issue by presenting data on people who have insecure food sources and suffer from some degree of hunger. It should be noted that homeless people are not included in these data. Therefore the number somewhat underestimates the problem. Calculate the percentage of people who suffer from some degree of hunger and place your answers in the appropriate spaces in the table.

6. How would you describe the trend you found in the data?

7. Which group has higher rates of hunger?

8. What factors contribute to this pattern?

TABLE 4.3   *Child Support Due and Received by Year (in thousands): 1993–1997*

Due Child Support	1993	1997
Child support due	6,685	7,006
Received full amount	2,280	2,863
Percent who received full amount		
Average amount due	$3,972	$4,152
Average amount received	$2,449	$2,440
Percent of amount due received		

Source: U.S. Census Bureau, *Child Support for Custodial Mothers and Fathers, 1997* (October 2000), pp. 60–212.

9. One issue related to higher rates of poverty and the accompanying potential for hunger is divorce. Children in single-parent families have a greater chance of living below poverty. Table 4.3 presents data on child support. The table includes information on how many custodial parents (those parents given custody of the children) are granted child support; how many receive the amount they were granted; and, what the actual amounts granted and received are. Calculate the percentage of children who actually receive the support that was granted, and then calculate the percentage of the awarded amount they received in full.

10. What observations can you make about the number of child-support payments that are received?

11. What observations can you make about the amount received?

12. How have both of these changed over time?

13. Why do you believe these changes have occurred?

TABLE 4.4   *All People and Children without Health Insurance for the Entire Year (in thousands): 1998 and 2001*

	2001			1998		
	Total No.	No. Uninsured	Percentage	Total No.	No. Uninsured	Percentage
All persons	282,082	41,207		271,743	44,281	
Under 18	72,628	8,509		72,022	11,073	
Under 6	23,373	2,503		23,665	3,671	
6 to 11	24,626	2,769		24,575	3,597	
12 to 17	24,629	3,237		23,782	3,805	

Source: U.S. Census Bureau, *Health Insurance Coverage: 1999.* www.census.gov/hhes/hlthins/hlthin99/ hi99ta.html; www.census.gov/hhes/hlthins/hlthin99/dtable-4.html; www.census.gov/hhes/hlthins/ hlthin01/tables.01.html

14. A final issue is health insurance. Given the high costs of medical care, health insurance, whether provided privately or through government programs, has become a necessity. However, not all Americans are covered by health insurance. Let us examine to what degree this is a problem for children. Table 4.4 presents data on the percentage of children who have no health insurance during the entire year. Calculate the percentage of all people and children without health insurance by age category.

15. What trend do you find in the data?

16. How would you interpret the statistic that 11.7 percent of all children under eighteen were not covered by any health insurance in 2001?

17. What policies or programs might you suggest to improve on the conditions noted in these data?

18. How do you believe these patterns affect the socialization of the children represented in these data?

Selected Bibliography and Suggested Readings _____

Ambart, A. M. (1997). *Parents, children, and adolescents: Interactive relationships and development in context.* New York: Haworth.

Baumrind, Diana. (1968). Authoritarian versus authoritative parental control. *Adolescence* 3, 255–272.

Cancian, F. M., & Oliker, S. (2000). *Caring and gender.* Lanham, MD: AltaMira.

Duncan, G., & Brooks-Gunn, J. (Eds.). (1997). *Consequences of growing up poor.* New York: Russell Sage.

Hernandez, Donald. (1993). *America's children.* New York: Russell Sage.

Erikson, Erik. (1963). *Childhood and society.* New York: W. W. Norton.

Logan, J., & Spitze, G. (1996). *Family ties: Enduring relations between parents and their grown children.* Philadelphia: Temple University Press.

Mead, George H. (1934). *Mind, self, and society.* Chicago: University of Chicago Press.

National Research Council. (1993). *Losing generations: Adolescents in high risk settings.* Washington, DC: National Academy Press.

Wilson, William J. (1997). *When work disappears: The world of the new urban poor.* New York: Alfred A. Knopf.

5

Little Boys and Girls: The Changing Nature of Gender

In the previous chapter one major aspect of socialization was omitted: the issue of gender socialization. Before discussing this basic process, two definitions are needed. Sometimes the terms *sex* and *gender* are used interchangeably. Social scientists, however, differentiate the two terms. **Sex** refers to the biological attributes with which one is born. Sex is the biological characteristics of the person. **Gender** refers to the social definitions associated with these biological characteristics.

The sex of a child is determined at conception. Without being too clinical, let me briefly explain how this takes place. All females' eggs contain an X chromosome. Males' sperm may be either an **X or Y chromosome.** If an X chromosome enters the egg, the child will be a female; if a Y chromosome enters the egg, the child will be a male. During the first six weeks after conception, the embryo has not yet developed male or female characteristics. At this point the embryo has the potential to be either male or female. In the sixth week, the Y chromosome creates changes in the embryo that will result in the development of male characteristics.

What is also important in the biological process is the action of certain hormones called **androgens.** One of these, **testosterone,** determines whether the child will be a male. If the male sex hormones are not present in sufficient amount the child will be a female. Interestingly, one may argue that all human beings are potentially female because an additional event has to happen for some of us to become male.

Although scientists do not have a full understanding of the relationship, the types of sex hormones produced by the embryo will influence brain functioning. There are slight differences in brain structure between males and females. These physiological differences raise questions about innate differences between boys and girls. This issue is often raised in the form of the **nature–nurture** controversy. *Nature* refers to biological and innate characteristics and nurture to the social environment.

It would be silly to think that there are no differences between males and females. Comedians have made a livelihood poking fun at some of these differences. The question is, how much of this difference can be attributed to biology and how much to upbringing? For example, research indicates that girls, in general, begin to talk earlier than boys. We also know that the left side of the brain is used to process language, and girls develop the use of the left side of their brain earlier than boys. Is this, then, the reason why girls talk earlier than boys? The answer is maybe "yes" and maybe "no." In studies of parent–child interactions, we find that parents talk more often to female children than they do to male children. Parents tend to be more verbal with girls and more physical with boys. Is it the verbal stimulation from the parent that results in girls talking sooner, or is it the result of the female sex hormones that influence brain functioning?

Let us look at another example. Boys are supposed to be more aggressive than girls. This aggressive tendency is often linked to the male hormone testosterone. Some research also indicates that girls who have an unusual amount of male hormones will be more aggressive than other girls with lesser amounts of these hormones. Aggression, however, may involve a wide range of behaviors. As noted above, parents tend to be more physical with boys than with girls. This physical play may be sending messages to boys that physical activity is expected and desired. Again, is the so-called aggressive tendency of boys biologically based or socially based? Is it nature or nurture?

Let us examine more closely the nurture side of this discussion. Look at the following list:

A	B
Nice	Tough
Sweet	Active
Cooperative	Competitive

If you were asked to decide which list represented boys and which list represented girls, how would you decide? There is little doubt that most, if not all of you, would select List A for girls and List B for boys. This is an example of **gender stereotyping.** Your response is not surprising because our culture has created dramatic differences in behavioral expectations. Men are supposed to be tough, active, and competitive, women nice, sweet, and cooperative. Children growing up in such a culture will tend to accept and internalize these stereotypic notions because such ideas tend to be transmitted from generation to generation.

This gender stereotyping is a result of the **gender norms** that exist in U.S. society. **Norms** are the expectations we have of each other. Gender norms, then, are the expectations we have of males and females. Gender norms, like all norms, involve three groups of expectations: expectations regarding how we feel, how we think, and how we behave. Let us look at each of these in turn.

With respect to feelings, our society expects different sets of emotions for males and females. By cultural definition, women are supposed to be emotional. They are free to express their emotions. On the other hand, men are supposed to suppress their feelings. This may be a vestige of our English cultural roots and the notion of "the stiff upper lip." "Real men" are not to express their feelings openly. Such behavior would be viewed as a weakness.

As for intellectual capabilities, here, too, U.S. culture clearly differentiates between males and females. Think of the notion of "female intuition." What does this really imply? It implies that women do not think rationally. That their way of seeing the world may include certain undefined mystical powers (intuition). These powers, however, are not based on reason or great intellectual ability. Men, on the other hand, are expected to think rationally and carefully plan out their actions.

Appropriate behavior is also defined by gender. Boys play with trucks and footballs, girls play with dolls. Boys get involved in rough play, girls do not. Boys are loud and boisterous; girls are quiet and demure. Interestingly, girls have some leeway with respect to their behavior. Girls who act boylike are called tomboys, and at least up to the preteen period this is somewhat acceptable. Boys, on the other hand, are never supposed to act girl-like. If such were to occur, the specter of homosexuality and a homophobic response might result. Family and friends may manifest great concern about the unmanlike behavior.

How do boys and girls come to learn these norms? One easy way to answer this question is to say that they learn it everywhere! To be more specific, children learn gender roles where they learn everything else: parents, extended kin, peer groups, mass media, and even the schools they attend. Research indicates that even the earliest parent–child interactions are influenced by the child's sex. From the color the parents paint the child's room, to the toys they give the child, to the types of interaction with respect to the use of physical or verbal play are all subject to the gender norms of the society. Extended kin will reinforce these actions.

Peer groups play a very important role in one's social development, and these groups also reinforce gender norms. Researchers have examined how same-sex play groups interact and they find that girl groups and boy groups interact in distinctly different ways, ways that reflect the gender norms of society. Boys play in a much more physical manner while girls' play tends to be more conversational. Research also indicates that the awareness of gender differences occurs early in one's development, perhaps as early as two to three years of age.

As an example of this early differentiation, I would like to add a personal anecdote. When my two children, both boys, were quite young, I sat with them watching a children's television show. As a point of information, I will tell you that both my wife and I work. We both shared in child-rearing responsibilities, and we often shared in household responsibilities as well. As best as I could tell we never defined our activities by gender. As we sat watching the show, a commercial showing some dolls came on. Both of my sons (both under the age of five) said, almost in unison: "Oh, we have to buy that doll for Mom." As best as I can remember, the commercial showed both boys and girls playing with the dolls. Where did they get the message about dolls and girls? Even at that early age, they had obviously gotten the message from somewhere. This is a good example of how gender norms permeate society, and, even in cases when parents do not wish to raise their children along traditional gender lines, there are many other sources of information that are gender-based.

This anecdote points to a third major source of gender norms and that is the **mass media.** Not just television, but books, movies, and even popular music can reinforce traditional notions of gender. Think of movies, for example. Are there any female counterparts to Arnold Schwarzenegger? Does Julia Roberts have a male counterpart? From its earliest days movies were made with male and female stars who represented the idealized cultural versions of masculinity and femininity.

Schools also help to shape the gender identity of girls and boys. There has been substantial research showing the differential treatment boys and girls receive in school. At least in the past boys were steered toward "male subjects" such as math and science. Girls were steered away from the same subjects. Ironically, many of the teachers who reinforced these stereotypic behaviors were women. There is no evidence to suggest that there are significant intellectual differences between males and females. Educational outcomes seem to be much more influenced by gender-differentiated opportunity structures.

If one looks at recent educational and occupational trends, there is a growing convergence of outcomes. More specifically, women are attaining the same level of education as men, and are also entering what had been traditional male occupations such as law, medicine, and accounting. There appears to be change in other areas as well. More young girls are in softball leagues and soccer leagues. There are women's teams in basketball from the elementary school level to a professional women's basketball league. There seem to be more parents who don't want their daughter to be a nurse; rather, they want her to become a doctor.

What then can be said about the issue first raised at the beginning of this chapter: the nature–nurture debate? Sex is clearly a biological variable. One is born with a penis or a vagina. It should be pointed out, however, that in a few cases, because of atypical development patterns in the fetus, a clear determination of sex cannot be made. For the most part though, sex is clearly defined at birth as a result of the XX or XY chromosome pair at conception.

It has also been pointed out that there are some characteristics that may be linked to sex, such as the earlier development of speech in girls. Research, however, indicates that the variations between the sexes are relatively small and not nearly as large as variations within either sex. Also, very often comparisons between groups are made in averages, and utilizing averages often overstates the differences that really exist. Averages also tell us nothing about in-group variations. Averages, perhaps most importantly, tell us nothing about any one individual in a group.

Biology, it seems, creates broad parameters but does not determine, in absolute terms, our outcomes. Our social environment influences much of our behavior, including our intellectual development. Even what constitutes intelligence or success is largely defined by the culture. Girls may be seen as weaker or inferior because others define them that way. What appears to be occurring today in the United States and elsewhere is that growing numbers of women are no longer accepting these definitions, and growing numbers of men and women are creating new definitions of gender.

The analysis section includes data on education, earnings, marital status, and life expectancy. From these data, you will be able to analyze how culture may influence selected gender differences.

Analysis

TABLE 5.1 *Percentage of College Graduates by People 25 Years Old and over by Sex (in thousands): 1960–2000*

| Year | Males | | | Females | | |
	Total No. Males	No. of College Graduates	Percent	Total No. Females	No. of College Graduates	Percent
2000	83,611	23,252		91,620	21,594	
1980	61,389	12,382		69,020	9,362	
1960	47,997	4,626		51,468	2,991	

Source: Adapted from U.S. Census Bureau, *Years of School Completed by People 25 Years Old and Over, by Age and Sex: Selected Years 1940 to 2000.* www.census.gov/population/socdemo/education/tableA-1.txt

1. First, examine some of the differences in educational attainment over time. Table 5.1 presents data on the number of college graduates by sex. Calculate the percentage of college graduates for males and females in the years shown and put your answers in the table.

2. What overall pattern emerges from your calculations?

3. How would you compare the changes for the males and the females?

4. What values or norms related to gender have contributed to the changes in educational attainment?

TABLE 5.2   *Median Weekly Earnings of Full-Time Wage and Salary Workers by Educational Level and Sex, 25 Years and Over: 2000*

Educational Level	Female Earnings	Male Earnings	Female–Male Ratio
Less than a high school diploma	303	409	
High school graduates, no college	421	594	
Some college or associate degree	504	699	
College graduates	760	1,022	.74

Source: Adapted from U.S. Department of Labor, Bureau of Labor Statistics, *Highlights of Women's Earnings in 2000,* Report 952, August 2001.

5. Educational attainment is related to income. Table 5.2 presents data on median weekly earnings by level of educational attainment. Remember that a **median** is the midpoint in a set of numbers. If the median weekly earnings for all female college graduates is $760, then 50 percent of all females earn more than this amount and 50 percent of all females earn less.

We can compute a ratio to get a better sense of the difference in female–male earnings. This is simple to do. All you have to do is divide the female earnings by the male earnings. For example, if you look at the earnings of college graduates you can use the following formula:

$$760/1022 = .743 \text{ or } \$.074$$

This would be interpreted as follows: female college graduates earn 74 cents on the dollar as compared to male college graduates. Now do the same calculation for all the levels of educational attainment and write your answers in the table.

6. What general pattern do you observe from the data?

7. How is educational attainment related to differences in earnings?

TABLE 5.3 *Median Weekly Earnings of Full-Time Wage and Salary Workers by Age and Sex: 2000*

Age	Female Earnings	Male Earnings	Female–Male Ratio
16 to 24	342	376	
25 to 34	493	603	
35 to 44	520	731	
45 to 54	565	777	
55 to 64	505	738	
65 and over	378	537	

Source: Adapted from U.S. Department of Labor, Bureau of Labor Statistics, *Highlights of Women's Earnings in 2000,* Report 952, August 2001.

8. Next, examine how the variable of age may impact on income differences. Table 5.3 presents median weekly wages by age. As you did in Table

5.2, calculate the ratios, this time by the variable of age and put your answers in the table.

9. How is the variable of age related to the differences in earnings?

10. What factors contribute to this pattern?

TABLE 5.4 *Median Weekly Earnings of Full-Time Wage and Salary Workers by Marital Status and Sex: 2000*

Marital Status	Female Earnings	Male Earnings	Female–Male Ratio
Never married	436	478	
Married, spouse present	517	735	
Divorced	509	650	
Separated	421	517	
Widowed	443	624	

Source: Adapted from U.S. Department of Labor, Bureau of Labor Statistics, *Highlights of Women's Earnings in 2000,* Report 952, August 2001.

11. Look at one more variable as it is related to earnings, marital status. Again, calculate the ratios in the same way you did in (5) and (8) and put your answers in Table 5.4.

12. Briefly describe the different ratios you found.

13. What might account for the differences in the ratios?

TABLE 5.5 *Life Expectancy at Birth by Sex: 1970–1999*

Year	Females	Males	Difference
1970	74.7	67.1	
1980	77.4	70.0	
1990	78.8	71.8	
1999	79.7	74.1	

Source: U.S. National Center for Health Statistics, *National Vital Statistics Report*, 48, 18 (February 7, 2001); U.S. Census Bureau, *Statistical Abstract of the United States: 2001*, Table 96.

14. So far this chapter has examined some of the socioeconomic consequences of gender with respect to educational and economic outcomes. As a last topic we will briefly examine one biological consequence of gender. Table 5.5 presents data on **life expectancy,** how long a person may expect to live given current mortality rates. Examine the data in the table and calculate, by simple subtraction, the difference in life expectancy for males and females. Put your answers in the table.

15. What has happened to the difference in life expectancy over the past thirty years?

16. What factors might help to explain this trend?

17. After examining all of the data in the analysis section of this chapter, what impact does gender have on the lives of men and women?

Selected Bibliography and Suggested Readings _____

Banner, Lois. (1983). *American beauty.* New York: Knopf.

Bernard, Jessie. (1981). *The female world.* New York: Free Press.

Gilbert, Susan. (2000). *A field guide to boys and girls.* New York: HarperCollins.

Harris, Judith. (1998). *The nurture assumption: Why children turn out the way they do.* New York: Free Press.

Kimura, Doreen. (2001). Sex differences in the brain. In Kathleen Gilbert (Ed.), *The family, 0102: Annual editions* (pp. 29–34). Guildford, CT: McGraw-Hill/Dushkin.

Kindlon, Daniel, Thompson, Michael, & Barker, Teresa. (1999). *Raising Cain: Protecting the emotional life of boys.* New York: Ballantine Books.

Lindsey, Linda. (1997). *Gender roles: A sociological perspective.* Upper Saddle River, NJ: Prentice-Hall.

Macoby, Eleanor, & Jacklin, Carol. (1974). *The psychology of sex differences.* Palo Alto, CA: Stanford University Press.

Orenstein, Peggy. (1994). *School girls: Young women, self-esteem, and the confidence gap.* New York: Doubleday.

Pollack, William. (1998). *Real boys: Rescuing our sons from the myths of boyhood.* New York: Random House.

Tanenbaum, Leora. (1999). *Slut! Growing up female with a bad reputation.* New York: Seven Stories Press.

Weitz, Shirley. (1977). *Sex roles: Biological, psychological, and social foundations.* New York: Oxford University Press.

6

Divorce: The End of the Affair

One of the most widely discussed domestic issues in the United States today is the issue of divorce. This is not surprising given the fact that divorce has risen dramatically since the early 1960s. This chapter will explore some of the reasons for the rise in divorce and the processes people go through when they experience divorce. The analysis section will allow you to examine the extent of divorce and changes in divorce over time as well as how many children are affected by divorce.

It is generally believed that one-half of all couples who marry will experience divorce. This is not completely accurate. Divorce, itself, is difficult to measure because people are getting married today and people are getting divorced today. They are not the same people. Therefore it is difficult to measure divorce at any one point in time. The 50 percent divorce rate may best be seen as a **projection.** A projection is an estimate of what will happen in the future. Experts in the field believe that, in the future, if current trends continue, 50 percent of all marriages will end in divorce. Notice the important phrase "if current trends continue." This is a major assumption, so one should be careful about making projections about divorce in the future. This should not be misconstrued. There is no question that the divorce rate is greater today than in the past. (You will analyze these data later on in the chapter.)

What factors help to explain the increase in divorce over the past forty years? There is no simple explanation. The increase is due to a combination of what may be viewed as **social and individual factors.** Let us examine some of the social factors first.

One important social factor that may have influenced the increase in divorce is the idea that marriages are no longer seen as a **sacred contract.** Historically, in many cultures, many aspects of life were dominated by religious beliefs. The marriage contract was seen as sacred, so there was little opportunity to sever the contract. (Even though this is true, it is interesting to note that all cultures do allow for some escape from marriage. That is, in all cultures there is some legitimate way to end a marriage.) To return to the main point, today, marriage is not seen by many as a sacred contract. While it is true that many people who marry still have a religious ceremony, this ceremony may occur because of its symbolic importance. Religion does not dictate their day-to-day behavior, and may not even influence their day-to-day beliefs. As with many other aspects of life, religion does not have much affect on how decisions are made. Therefore, the notion that divorce may be "sinful" is not as prominent as it once was, and sin is no longer an effective deterrent to divorce.

Related to this decline in religious commitment is the fact that marriage is seen as a **voluntary contract** entered into by two independent persons. In the past marriage was very much entwined with the larger community. In many cultures, marriages were seen as forging alliances between two families, not just between two individuals, so it was more difficult to obtain a divorce because it involved separating two families. Today, because marriage is an individual contract, if two individuals no longer wish to be married, they believe they have the right to terminate the marriage.

A third social factor that may have led to increases in divorce rates is the **changing nature of family life.** In the past family life was the center of all activity. Families lived together and worked together. While this is almost incomprehensible to most people today, in the past family members spent very little time away from each other. Today, people wake up in the morning, the wife goes off to her job, the husband goes off to his, and the children go off to school. They may get together in the evening for dinner. However, because of the shifting nature of work schedules, and children with their after-school activities, even the family evening meal may be a thing of the past. In a sense there are fewer connections that hold husbands and wives together, and there may be a decline in the activities family members share with each other.

A fourth major social factor is the **changing role of women.** Women, in most cultures, derive their status from the man they marry. Women have been emotionally and financially tied to their husbands. Wife and mother were the two highest statuses that women could claim. Today, much of this has changed. Women, through changing educational and occupational patterns, now have achieved a greater sense of self-identity independent of any male. Women do not have to be tied to a male in order to have a sense of place in society. As a result, women who find themselves in unsatisfactory marriages are more willing emotionally, and more capable in practical terms, to end the relationship.

A last social factor that influences divorce is **social class.** Divorce has certainly become more "democratic" over the past forty years. By democratic, I mean that divorce appears to occur across the board in terms of the population's characteristics. People from all social classes, racial, ethnic, and religious groups experience divorce. Divorce, however, does exhibit certain patterns. Specifically, there appears to be a correlation between social class and divorce. It is a widely held belief that the rich have a higher divorce rate than the rest of the population. This is untrue. What may account for this belief is the fact that, when a wealthy person divorces, it is a headline in the newspaper or on the evening television news program. When poor people divorce, it does not make the news. The data indicate that divorce is more widespread in the lower social classes. This should come as no surprise. Poor people lack resources and may be more vulnerable to a variety of stressful situations, such as marital stress, that result from financial exigencies.

Individual factors also influence divorce. One of the strongest predictors of divorce is **age at marriage.** As with social class, there is a strong correlation between marrying at an early age and eventual divorce. This is especially true if one of the partners is eighteen years of age or younger. Obviously, people need some level of maturity to make such an important decision, and maturity generally comes with age. Young people may not have enough experience to make such important decisions.

Another factor is **love at first sight.** Romantic notions aside, people do not fall in love at first sight. Love is a process that emerges over time. Love at first sight is more likely to be a physical and/or sexual attraction, and attraction is different from love. Young people, especially teenagers, often confuse the two. Sexual attraction and sexuality are part of a mature loving relationship, but they are not the same as love.

Having a **brief courtship period** before marrying can also lead to divorce. It takes time to get to know another person. It is necessary to see the person in a variety of situations, in a variety of social settings, and in a variety of social interactions in order to understand what someone is really like. A brief relationship does not allow a couple to really get to know one another, so it is not surprising that couples who have had relatively short relationships may have higher rates of divorce.

Differences in background can also lead to divorce. Here, differences in background mean class, religious, ethnic, or educational differences, but it can also include differences in values, beliefs, and goals. There is an old expression that "opposites attract." Research, by the way, indicates that this is not necessarily the case. Researchers have found that people are attracted to others who are similar to them. Opposites may attract, but they rarely date, and they almost never marry. If they do marry, they also have higher rates of divorce.

The social and individual factors discussed above are some, but certainly not all, predictors of divorce. A word of caution is needed. These factors should not be seen in absolute terms. In social science, it is difficult to ascertain clear relationships of causality. We can state that, if a person under the age of eighteen marries, then there is a greater chance for divorce. However, there are a number of married couples who married at an early age, who have been married for a very long period of time, and who, by all accounts, are very happily married. The presence of these factors does not in any way "guarantee" that certain marriages will fail. In the same vein, the absence of these predictors does not ensure the success of a marriage. The presence or absence of any or all of these factors guarantees nothing.

Having examined some of the factors that may result in divorce, let us next look at divorce itself. Paul Bohannan, an anthropologist, some years ago presented an analysis of divorce as involving six subprocesses (see the Selected Bibliography and Suggested Readings at the end of this chapter).

A number of people believe that individuals who decide to divorce have not taken their marriages seriously, and that most people find divorce easy. In most instances, this is not the case. Divorce is a complex, multilayered process. It is often emotionally draining, financially burdensome, and stressful on a multitude of levels. According to Bohannan, there are six processes that occur coincidental to each other during the divorce process: the emotional divorce, the legal divorce, the economic divorce, the parental divorce, the community divorce, and the psychic divorce.

While almost all the processes occur simultaneously, **the emotional divorce** chronologically comes first. If marriage is seen as a selection process, then the emotional divorce involves a de-selection process. The emotional divorce begins to occur when one partner in the marriage begins to feel a distancing from the other party. This may begin as slight feelings of misgiving. It may emerge from a variety of vague feelings of discontent. There is no set time limit for this process. In fact, it is very possible that there are a number of individuals who go through an emotional divorce but never get divorced. These negative feelings toward the other may lead to a strong sense of guilt. The individual may deny her or his own feelings and cannot come to accept the idea of divorce and so may never say to the other "I want a divorce."

Let us assume, however, that this emotional divorce does eventually lead to an open declaration. How might that happen? It certainly is possible for someone to confront another with these feelings. I think, however, that for many people the process is subtler, and they may begin to give hints or cues about their internal feelings. The other person may see these cues, but find them too threatening, so go into denial, refusing to see what he or she doesn't wish to see. This "dance" may go on for some time. As noted before, it may never end, or it may lead to the eventual confrontation/discussion about divorce.

To some degree, the emotional divorce never ends. It will continue throughout the divorce and, as we will see, make the other processes more difficult. Once the topic of divorce is explicit between the two partners the next process to emerge is the **legal divorce.** Each state has its own set of laws regarding marriage and divorce. There are no federal laws regarding the marriage and divorce. The marriage license is a legal contract. In order to break this contract, one must go through the legal process called divorce. Although most people don't think about this, it is much easier to enter this particular contract than it is to break it. It is one of the ironies of the divorce process.

The legal divorce has undergone substantial change since Bohannan wrote his original essay. Prior to the 1970s, divorce in all states, with one exception, involved what was termed an **adversarial process.** This meant that one party had to be found guilty of some wrongdoing or some legally acceptable reason for getting the divorce. For example, let us say that it's 1950 and Mr. and Mrs. X have had the divorce conversation. They come to see that they have grown apart from one another and neither partner wishes to remain married. They do not hate each other. They have not abused each other. They have simply grown distant. They both agree on the divorce. They go to their respective lawyers and explain the situation. The lawyers then contact each other and try to create legally acceptable reasons to present to the court so their clients can get a divorce. The problem was that the scenario just presented would not lead to the granting of a divorce. The lawyers literally had to make something up such as "mental cruelty." Understand that no mental cruelty existed in this hypothetical relationship, but before a judge the parties would have to commit perjury in order to be granted the divorce.

In many states today divorce law has moved toward **no-fault divorce.** This would allow our Mr. and Mrs. X to get a divorce without committing perjury. They could go before a judge and claim that there were "irreconcilable differences," a much more neutral term that does not imply blame. This is not to suggest that legal divorces are easy to get. In some instances, they are if both parties agree. In fact, in some instances one can get a divorce by using materials published on the Internet. In many cases, however, divorces can still be quite trying and involve substantial amounts of conflict. In some states, the courts are so backlogged with cases that some parties have to wait three years to have their cases heard by the court. Overall, what may be the most accurate observation about the legal divorce is that it is easier to get now than in the past, but this does not mean it is easy.

A major component of the legal divorce is the **economic divorce.** Marriages are not only legal entities; they are also economic entities. In some ways marriages are like corporations or legal partnerships. Marriages have assets and they have liabilities. During the divorce process there needs to be an accounting of the economic worth of the marriage. The liabilities have to be paid off and the remaining assets have to be divided.

Understand that this occurs while the emotional divorce is still going on, and material objects may sometimes take on an emotional value beyond their actual worth. For example, let us say the couple has a couch that neither one of them ever liked. They do not even know what made them purchase it in the first place. Now they come to the divorce, and emotions run very high. Each one feels that they *must* have that couch because they do not want the other party to get it.

At the same time, the attorneys may be important players in the economic divorce. Attorneys make their reputations by winning cases.

In divorce law, getting the best possible settlements for their clients makes their reputations, so each attorney has a vested interest in "winning" the economic divorce. These factors may come together to make divorces drag on for an extended period of time. (The economic impact of divorce will be discussed further in the chapter on single parenting, Chapter 12.)

Of all the elements involved in divorce the one that has received the most attention and concern is its impact on children. This is the **parental divorce.** The presence of children complicates the entire divorce process and affects all the other processes we are examining in this section. The presence of children will exacerbate the legal and economic discussions most dramatically.

There is no consensus as to the short-term or long-term effects of divorce on children. Some research indicates that there are substantially negative long-term effects, and that even adult children of divorced parents suffer from their parents' divorce experience. On the other hand, some research indicates that negative effects can be relatively short-lived, and, after some period of time, may no longer be felt.

There is a general consensus that a variety of factors will influence the nature of the child's reaction to divorce. **Age** is one such factor. In very young children there is less of an impact than in teenagers. The **sex** of the child can also be important. Research indicates that for both male and female children there are negative consequences, but the consequences may be worse for males. This may be related to the fact that in most cases the mother becomes the custodial parent, and boys may have negative experiences because their fathers are absent from the home. This, of course, assumes that the father was a positive force in the son's life prior to the divorce.

The **marital relationship** may be another factor in how children react to divorce. If the parents had an embattled and bitter marriage, the divorce may come as a relief for the children because they may no longer have to witness battles being fought between their parents. Divorce may bring with it a kind of closure for the child. What is also important here is the **post-marital relationship.** What is the nature of the relationship between the parents after the divorce? If the parents are still in a state of conflict, then the post-divorce period may be as stressful as the divorce was. If, on the other hand, after the divorce the parents come to have a civil and mutually supportive relationship that focuses on the well-being of the child, then the child may adjust in a much healthier manner.

Divorces do not occur in a social vacuum. Married couples are part of a larger community. There are extended kin and friends who may be affected by the divorce. This is referred to as the **community divorce.** Mother-in-law jokes aside, there are many instances when people develop close relationships with a spouse's relatives. How does one adjust to these relationships in the post-divorce period? There are no rules or norms regarding the nature of these relationships. Do you maintain contact, or do you sever the relationship completely? Do you try to maintain some type of continuing relationship, albeit one that will be quite different than the one you had prior to the divorce? People outside the divorce may feel a real sense of loss because of the divorce.

The last subprocess is the **psychic divorce.** There is nothing mystical about this process, so I prefer the term the *individual divorce.* For many people going through the divorce process, this may be the most difficult process to complete successfully. Individuals begin their relationship by dating, after some period of time they marry, and then they are married. Throughout this period they create what I call a sense of "we-ness." Even in their day-to-day language they may come to use the pronoun *we* rather than the pronoun *I.* "We will go shopping. We will stay home. We will go out to a movie." This is not at all unusual, and is probably the norm for most married couples.

Throughout the divorce process, and certainly after the legal divorce is completed, there will be a need to come to terms with one's *"I"-ness.* This is not merely a matter of language. It is a matter of personal identity. For X number of years the person has seen himself or herself as a member of a partnership. That partnership has now been severed. One can view this as a process of separation and renewal, but this transition may be very difficult to achieve. Regardless of whether or not the marital relationship was a good one or not, there still may be stress in coming to terms with this new identity. Apart from the legal and economic issues, the psychological issues may also be problematic. It is not unusual for people to feel depressed and anxious with this new persona of "I," and there may be a need to evaluate who one is and where one is going. It may be argued that once the individual is capable of creating a strong sense of self, the divorce process has been successfully completed.

In the analysis section the reader will have the opportunity to examine changes in divorce rates over time, and how there have been changes in the number of children affected.

Analysis

TABLE 6.1 *Marriages and Divorces by Year: 1980–1998*

Year	Marriages	Divorces
1980	2,390	1,189
1990	2,443	1,182
1998	2,244	1,135

Source: U.S. Census Bureau, *Statistical Abstract of the United States: 2000,* Table 144.

1. First, examine the actual number of divorces in the United States. Table 6.1 presents data on marriages and divorces. For marriages, what is the percent change between 1980 and 1990? _____

1990 and 1998? _____

1980 and 1998? _____

2. What has been the percentage change for divorces from 1980 to 1990?

_____

1990 to 1998? _____

1980 to 1998? _____

3. For both marriages and divorces, what pattern seems to be emerging?

4. What reasons can you give for the emergence of this pattern?

TABLE 6.2   *Refined Divorce Rates by Sex (in thousands): 1950 to 2000*

Year	Males			Females		
	Married	*Divorced*	*Rate*	*Married*	*Divorced*	*Rate*
2000	59,684	8,572	144	60,527	11,309	
1990	55,833	6,283		56,797	8,845	
1980	51,813	3,930		52,965	5,966	
1970	47,109	1,567		48,148	2,717	
1960	41,781	1,106		42,583	1,708	
1950	36,866	1,071		37,577	1,373	

Source: U.S. Census Bureau, *Current Population Reports,* Series P20, No. 514, Internet release data: January 7, 1999; www.census.gov/population/socdemo/ms-la/tabms-1.txt and update (June 29, 2001); www.census.gov/population/socdemo/hh-fam/tabms-1.txt

5. Table 6.1 presents what is called raw data on marriages and divorces. Raw data are the actual number of marriages and divorces. In analyzing data researchers often try to develop more refined measures that allow for a clearer analysis of the subject they are studying. We can create a refined measure by comparing married and divorced people. This may be considered "refined" because only married people can get divorced. Therefore we are focusing in on the at-risk population. The formula is as follows:

$$\frac{\text{Divorced persons}}{\text{Married persons}} \times 1,000 = \begin{array}{l}\text{No. of divorced persons} \\ \text{for every 1,000 married persons}\end{array}$$

For example, in Table 6.2, in 2000 there were 59,684,000 married males and 8,572,000 divorced males. If you divide the divorced figure by the married figure and multiply by 1,000, your answer will be 144. This means that, for every 1,000 married males in 2000, there were 144 divorced males. This number has been placed in the table for you. Now calculate the other rates indicated in Table 6.2 and put your answers in the table.

6. What patterns do you find from your calculations?

7. What factors do you believe contribute to the pattern you discovered?

TABLE 6.3 *Number of Children under 18 Years Living with a Divorced Parent (in thousands): 1960 to 1998*

Year	Total No. of Children	Living with Mother	Percent	Living with Father	Percent	Total Living with Divorced Parent
2000	72,012	5,655		1,330		
1990	64,137	5,118		1,004		
1980	63,427	4,766		515		
1970	69,162	2,296		177		
1960	63,727	1,210		129		

Source: U.S. Census Bureau, *Current Population Reports,* P-20, No. 514 and earlier;
www.census.gov/population/socdemo/ms-la/tabch-1.txt
www.census.gov/population/socdemo/ms-la/tabch-5.txt
www.census.gov/population/socdemo/ms-la/tabch-6.txt
www.census.gov/population/socdemo/hh-fam/tab (ch-1.txt,ch-5.txt, and ch-6.txt)

8. One major issue related to divorce is parenting. A large number of children may be raised by one parent because of divorce. Table 6.3 presents

data on the number of children living with divorced parents, either their mother or father. Calculate the percentage of children living with either their mother or father. Then, combine the percentages you've calculated to see the total percentage of children living with a divorced parent. Put your answers in the table.

9. Describe the pattern you find for children living with divorced mothers.

10. Describe the pattern you find for children living with divorced fathers and mothers.

11. Why do you believe this occurred?

12. Which period had the greatest increase for children living with divorced fathers and mothers?

13. Why do you believe this occurred?

14. Based on the data analyzed in this chapter, what general conclusions can be drawn about divorce in the United States today?

Selected Bibliography and Suggested Readings _____

Ahrons, Constance. (1994). *The good divorce: Keeping your family together when your marriage comes apart.* New York: HarperCollins.

Amato, P., & Booth, A. (1997). *A generation at risk: Growing up in an era of family upheaval.* Cambridge, MA: Harvard University Press.

Bohannan, Paul. (Ed.). (1971). *Divorce and after.* Garden City: Anchor.

Furstenberg, Frank, & Cherlin, Andrew. (1991). *Divided families: What happens to the children when parents part.* Cambridge, MA: Harvard University Press.

Goode, William. (1993). *World changes in divorce patterns.* New Haven, CT: Yale University Press.

Hackstaff, Karla. (1999). *Marriage in a culture of divorce.* Philadelphia: Temple University Press.

Hetherington, E. Mavis, & Kelly, John. (2002). *For better or for worse.* New York: Norton.

Mason, M. (1999). *Custody wars: Why children are losing the legal battle and what we can do about it.* New York: Basic Books.

Parkman, A. (2000). *Good intentions gone awry: No-fault divorce and the American family.* Lanham, MD: Rowman and Littlefield.

Wallerstein, J., Blakeslee, Sandra, & Lewis, Julia. (2000). *The unexpected legacy of divorce: A 25-year landmark study.* New York: Hyperion.

7

Family Violence: Lost Innocence

Our ideal image of the family presents it as a warm, loving group without any conflict or violence. Unfortunately, reality does not always match this image. Families, it seems, have always been arenas of violence. Even the Old Testament offers accounts of family violence. There is **fratricide**, the killing of one's brother, as told in the story of Cain and Abel. There is the attempted murder of a child in the story of Abraham and Isaac. There is incest between Lot and his daughters. Jacob has sexual relations with his daughter-in-law.

In more recent times, family historians suggest that there was substantial family violence during the nineteenth century. **Infanticide**, the killing of infants was not uncommon in nineteenth-century England, and abandonment of children was not unusual in Europe or the United States. Even the values of the past seem to support what we might call violence today. The famous American aphorism, "Spare the rod and spoil the child," illustrates a value system that approves of corporal punishment. In the past, physical punishment was an indication of good parenting. The use of physical force against children, and in many cases wives, was not uncommon.

Even today discussions and debates continue about **spanking**. Defenders of spanking see it as a perfectly acceptable form of punishment, a method to avoid "spoiling" the child ("spare the rod" again). Supporters argue that spanking teaches the child to be obedient and to respect their elders. Critics see spanking as a rationalized form of abuse, as demeaning the child, and treating the child in an unfair and inhumane manner.

It is my view that spanking teaches the child to spank! The message being sent to the child is that, under certain circumstances, as defined by the person in power, it is all right to use physical force. This raises a larger point related to parenting. Parents use certain techniques to communicate values and beliefs to their children. When parents spank they believe they are teaching their children right from wrong. What is actually taught is that violence is an acceptable method to use in social interaction. Parents are thus communicating something that they may not wish to communicate. This is not the only case when this can occur. Sending messages to children you do not intend may be somewhat common in parent–child relations. This happens to be one of the more dramatic instances of the phenomenon.

With respect to family violence, what was acceptable in the past appears to be no longer acceptable today, with the possible exception of the aforementioned spanking issue. Many people believe that family violence is more widespread today than in the past. There is no evidence to suggest that this is the case. In fact, given the historical evidence, one may surmise that family violence may be less prevalent today. What appears to have changed is how people perceive it. Family violence has now become news. It has come to be defined as deviant, and in many instances as criminal.

How did this change in perception come about? Although it is difficult to pinpoint a specific date for the change, evidence seems to suggest that the changing perception of violence occurred sometime between the mid-1950s and the mid-1960s. The changing perception was a result of a number of factors that came together during this time period.

The first major influence on the attitudinal shift was the Negro Civil Rights Movement, the attempt by African Americans to achieve full equal rights in U.S. society. Starting at the turn of the twentieth century, and coming to a full flowering after World War II, this movement culminated in major Supreme Court decisions that defined segregation and discrimination as unconstitutional. This movement focused on the notion of equal rights. Once one group advocates for equal rights, it is not surprising that the idea spreads to other groups as well. If African Americans should be accorded fair and equal treatment, what then about women? What about children? If African Americans should not be subject to maltreatment, shouldn't this value hold for everyone? Thus, the civil rights movement became a model for attacking issues of intimate and family violence.

A second factor contributing to the changing perception of family violence was the growing awareness of violence in general. By the mid-1950s the United States had engaged in two major world wars and a military conflict in Korea. In the early 1960s, United States involvement in Vietnam began to expand and by 1965 the Vietnam War was the headline news story almost every evening. Consequently, the public's consciousness was raised with respect to violence in general. The increasing involvement in Vietnam led to more domestic violence in the form of anti-war protests. At the same time, protests in African American communities increased over frustration that the civil rights legislation did not achieve what they hoped for. Violence now became a topic for everyday discussion. As with the notion of civil rights, once people start thinking about violence, they begin to think about violence in other venues.

A third factor that influenced the changing perception of family violence was the development of interest in selected professional communities. More specifically, social workers, psychologists, and others began to take an interest in this area. Research articles and books began to be published on the subject, which increased the public's awareness. Sociologists, too, began to play a major role in this shift and undertook major studies of family violence. Even within the discipline, there was an increase in the use of **conflict theory** and **gender roles** as foci for study. Conflict theory examines the role of conflict in society. Conflict theorists argue that conflict is always a potential in society, and contributes to societal change. The study of gender roles examines how society defines what it means to be male and female (see Chapter 5). Both of these helped to shape the study of family violence over the past thirty years.

As a result of the work of large numbers of researchers, we now know much more about family violence than was known in the past. Before I go any further, a caveat. While our knowledge has increased incrementally, there is still much we do not know. What follows is a general summary of our understanding up to this time. The reader should understand that there is still much we need to know.

One thing we do know is that family violence includes a wide range of behaviors. When people think of family violence, what often comes first to their mind is physical violence, one of the behaviors regarded as family violence. Physical force causing pain and anguish is one category of violence, but there are others, including such behaviors as threatening physical abuse, demeaning, verbal abuse, sexual abuse, neglect, and emotional abuse. Let me be a little more specific. Following is a list of behaviors that may indicate that one's partner is being abusive, but this list is not exhaustive.

- calls you names
- is overprotective
- humiliates or embarrasses family members
- controls all the finances
- threatens harm
- destroys personal property
- forces the other person to have sex
- uses physical force

In the attempt to explain why family violence occurs, two types of explanation emerge from the research: the **sociological** and the **individual.** The **sociological approach** tries to identify general social factors that contribute to family violence. First is what we call **social norm theory.** Does the society have norms that legitimate or have the potential to increase the probability of family violence? For example, is violence an acceptable means to resolve conflict? One of the major images in U.S. culture, and one reinforced by the mass media, is the gunfight at high noon. Two men engage in a conflict, and their resolution to that conflict is to have a duel. This cowboy image of manliness has two effects. First, *violence is a way to resolve conflict.* A second underlying theme is one of **patriarchy.** Women did not "shoot it out," men did. The message is that men have the right to use violence, women do not. Patriarchy has other important ramifications as a social system. In patriarchal societies men monopolize power. Women and children are often seen as the property of men, and, as with other property, men can do as they wish with them. Women and children are "owned." In such societies it is not difficult to see that there would be a greater potential for family violence.

The second sociological theory is **social resource theory.** Social resources refer to psychological and economic resources individuals may develop within a particular social setting. Does the society offer individuals the opportunity to develop these resources? **Psychological resources** include the notion of positive self-worth. Does the individual have the ability to resolve conflicts without resorting to violence? Can the person process anger and frustration or does the person have a need to lash out at others?

While this may be seen as an individual element, the social environment can play a role in contributing to the development of psychological resources. For example, are individuals given the opportunity to succeed? Is there opportunity for success in school, in the workplace, and in other arenas of interaction? If the society has an institutionalized system of discrimination based on race, class, ethnic, or gender characteristics then certain groups of individuals may be more prone to frustration and the resulting violent behavior. As an aside, the reader should note that this is not to suggest that violent behavior of any sort is justified. Rather, this is an attempt at explanation, the goal of scientific inquiry.

Related to psychological resources are the **economic resources.** The lack of economic resources can have a devastating effect on people. Poverty, for example, is associated with a variety of negative behaviors including violence. Economic problems are associated with higher levels of stress, and high levels of stress are related to a greater potential for violent behavior. As noted above, does the society allow for success in an economic sense? Are there equal opportunities for work? Are there equal opportunities to achieve some degree of economic well-being? These interact with the psychological resources to contribute to a general sense of positive or negative self-worth. While family violence does occur across social class lines, research does indicate that it is more prevalent among the lower social classes, and the more violent forms of family violence tend to occur among these groups.

The **individual approach** focuses on characteristics of people who perpetrate violence within the family. A number of researchers have come up with what one might call a checklist of characteristics. Although not exhaustive some of the characteristics often cited are:

- poor self-image
- refuses to accept responsibility for own actions
- very jealous and possessive
- projects blame onto others
- some degree of depression
- difficulty processing anger

There has also been a substantial amount of research on the victims of abuse. For wives and girlfriends, the following is a sample of the characteristics researchers have found. Again, the list is a sample and is not exhaustive of the information available.

- poor self-image
- fear of physical abuse even if they try to leave
- economic dependence on the male
- feel they have no means of escape and no place to go
- less education and fewer job skills
- shame and embarrassment at the thought of leaving

One problematic explanation for why victims remain in abusive relationships is called **blaming the victim.** Some people attribute blame to the victim herself, but research indicates that many victims are "trapped" by their circumstances and cannot find a way out of their abusive situation.

One characteristic that often appears in the literature is **social isolation.** Certainly not in all cases, but in many, both the perpetrator and the victim are socially isolated. In some instances the pattern is as follows: the perpetrator is a social isolate, he has few, if any friends, and perhaps has even lost contact with his own family. Over time he comes to isolate his mate/girlfriend so that she becomes disconnected from family and friends.

Since the accumulation of knowledge about family violence what has been done? Much has changed since the 1950s. From a scholarly perspective, there are many more sophisticated research techniques now in use to better understand the problem. There is child abuse legislation in all fifty states. Courts now accept "**the battered woman syndrome**" as a defense in cases where the victim of abuse uses aggressive behavior to defend herself. In most states, teachers must have special training that will give them the skills needed to identify potential victims of child abuse. Police officers and medical personnel also undergo special training so that they will be able to spot incidents of abuse.

While progress has been made in this area, many experts feel there is still much to be done. Children, women, and men are still being abused. Research has begun to examine the issue of sibling abuse, and elderly abuse also has become the subject of increasing levels of research. It is argued that there is still a need to confront and eliminate the norms that legitimate violence.

There is a need to try to reduce the social and economic patterns that increase levels of stress in people's lives. In order to reduce social isolation, policies are needed that allow for greater integration of families into communities.

Each year the Department of Justice publishes *The Uniform Crime Reports*. From this report a variety of data related to violent behavior can be extracted. The analysis section will give the reader the opportunity to analyze some of these data as they relate to family violence.

Analysis

TABLE 7.1   *Victim-to-Offender Relationships: All Violent Crimes, 1998*

Relationship	Number	Percent
Spouse	49,089	
Common-law spouse	10,554	
Parent	11,100	
Sibling	11,726	
Child	12,570	
Other family member	20,342	
Offender (family disputes where both husband and wife are charged)	24,360	
Otherwise known	234,126	
Stranger	59,229	
Unknown	58,993	
Total	492,079	

Source: U.S. Department of Justice. *Uniform Crime Reports, 1998.*

1. First, look at the number and percentage of family members who have been victims of violent incidents. Table 7.1 presents data on victim-to-offender relationships for all violent crimes committed in 1998. Calculate the percentage distribution of the crimes and put your answers in the table.

2. What percentage of all violent crimes involve some form of family relationship?

TABLE 7.2   *Type of Offense, Family Violence: 1998*

Offense	Number	Percent
Murder	205	
Forcible rape	1,380	
Robbery	153	
Aggravated assault	16,402	
Simple assault	80,689	
Intimidation	8,195	
Other offenses	5,081	
Total	112,042	

Source: U.S. Department of Justice. *Uniform Crime Reports, 1998.*

3. Next, examine the types of offenses that occur between family members. Table 7.2 categorizes these offenses. Calculate the percentage distribution by type of family violence and put your answers in the table.

4. Which offense has the highest number of cases?

5. Why do you think this is the most common offense?

TABLE 7.3   *Victim to Offender Relationship, Family Violence: 1998*

Relationship	Number	Percent
Spouse	49,089	
Common-law spouse	10,544	
Parent	11,100	
Sibling	11,726	
Child	12,570	
Grandparent	573	
Grandchild	762	
In-law	3,411	
Stepparent	1,957	
Stepchild	2,981	
Stepsibling	620	
Other family member	10,038	
Offender	24,360	
Total	139,731	

Source: U.S. Department of Justice. *Uniform Crime Reports, 1998.*

6. Within the family, who is most likely to be the victim of family violence? Table 7.3 presents data on the victims of family violence. Again, calculate the percentage distribution of victims and put your answers in the table.

7. How would you describe the pattern that emerges from the data?

8. Why do spouses account for such a large percentage of all victims?

TABLE 7.4   *Percentage Distribution of Murder Victims by Age and Sex: 1998*

	All Murders	*Murder in Families*
Age		
0–11	7.0	20.5
12–17	4.4	2.0
18 and over	85.0	74.6
Unknown	3.7	2.9
Sex		
Male	65.7	43.9
Female	33.6	55.6
Unknown	0.7	2.9

Source: U.S. Department of Justice. *Uniform Crime Reports, 1998.*

9. Table 7.4 presents data on murder. It analyzes the data by the percentage distribution of victims by age and sex, and it includes data for all murders and for murders that occur within families. What differences occur with respect to the age of the victims?

10. What differences occur with respect to the sex of the victim?

11. Why do you believe these differences appear in the data?

TABLE 7.5   *Percentage of Murders That Offenders Were Suspected of Substance Abuse: 1998*

Type of Substance	All Murders	Murders in Families
Alcohol	13.3	17.2
Drugs	3.2	3.4
Multiple	2.4	1.5
None	81.1	77.9
Total	100.0	100.0

Source: U.S. Department of Justice. *Uniform Crime Reports, 1998.*

12. Substance abuse is often seen as being a factor in family violence. As a last exercise, let us examine the role of drugs and alcohol in family violence. Again, we will look at the data for murder. Table 7.5 presents data on murder and the suspected involvement of drugs. As with Table 7.4, percentages are given for all cases of murder and for cases of murder within families. Do there appear to be significant differences in the involvement of substance abuse in cases of murder within families?

13. What role does substance abuse appear to play in cases of murder?

14. Based on the data you examined in this chapter, what general conclusions can be drawn about family violence today?

Selected Bibliography and Suggested Readings _____

Beck, Aaron. (1999). *Prisoners of hate: The cognitive basis of anger, hatred, and violence.* New York: HarperCollins.

Bergen, Raquel. (Ed.). (1998). *Issues in intimate violence.* Thousand Oaks, CA: Sage.

Cardarelli, A. (Ed.). (1997). *Violence between intimate partners.* Boston: Allyn & Bacon.

Cherlin, Andrew. (2002). *Public and private families: An introduction* (3rd ed.). Boston: McGraw-Hill. (See pp. 386–413.)

Cox, Frank. (2002). *Human intimacy: Marriage, the family, and its meaning* (9th ed.). Belmont, CA: Wadsworth. (See pp. 466–471.)

Gelles, R. (1997). *Intimate violence in families* (3rd ed.). Thousand Oaks, CA: Sage.

Hyman, Irwin. (1997). *The case against spanking: How to stop hitting and start raising healthy kids.* San Francisco: Jossey-Bass.

Jacobson, Neil, & Gottman, John. (1998). *When men batter women.* New York: Simon and Schuster.

Roberts, Albert. (2002). *Handbook of domestic violence intervention strategies: Policies, programs, legal remedies.* New York: Oxford University Press.

Straus, Murray. (1994). *Beating the devil out of them: Corporal punishment in American families.* San Francisco: Jossey-Bass.

Trickett, P., & Schellenbach, C. (Eds.). (1998). *Violence against children in the family and the community.* Washington, DC: American Psychological Association.

Utech, M. (1994). *Violence, abuse, and neglect: The American home.* Lanham, MD: AltaMira.

Zubretsky, Theresa. (1996). *Domestic violence: Finding safety and support.* Rensselaer, NY: New York State Office for the Prevention of Domestic Violence.

8

Singlehood: I'd Rather Not, Thank You Anyway

Marriage is highly valued in all societies. People, when they reach the appropriate age, as defined by the culture, are supposed to marry. In many cultures there is no place for a single adult. In fact, in many societies adult status is defined by marriage. There is some gender variation in this long-held view. Men typically marry at later ages and appear to have more flexibility in terms of when to marry. Women, on the other hand, are expected to marry young, and most cultures define the age at which they must marry. If they do not marry by that prescribed age, unmarried women are often seen as social pariahs. They are called old maids or worse. Even men living in patriarchal societies are not immune to being stigmatized if they do not marry. They may be viewed as bachelors, which does not have the negative connotation of old maid, but is certainly not looked on as the norm. An elderly bachelor is seen as somewhat odd, if not downright "eccentric." These strong promarriage views were reinforced by religious dogma. In all cultures marriage has a strong religious element, and there is widespread belief in the **sanctity of marriage** that cuts across religious lines.

It may seem somewhat surprising then that there has been a substantial change in marriage patterns over the past thirty years. More people are remaining single for longer periods of time. Even popular media reflect this shift. During the 1950s and 1960s, one of the main staples of evening television was the situation comedy in which the married couple was the focus. Today, more and more shows seem to have singles as their focus. Think of the show "Friends," for example.

While the mass media do not always reflect social reality, in this case the data appear to support the growing importance of a single lifestyle. If one examines the data over the past thirty years, as you will have the opportunity to do in the analysis section of this chapter, you will find dramatic changes in the number of singles. Before we go any further, a point of clarification needs to be made. Singles, of course, may include anyone who is not married: never-married people and divorced and widowed persons. For the sake of this chapter, singles will be only those people who are never married.

If we look at the data for people thirty to thirty-four years of age, we find a dramatic change in the proportion that has never married. In 1970, almost 8 percent of people in their early thirties had never married, about one out of twelve people. Most people were expected to marry, and certainly most people were expected to marry by the time they reached thirty-five years of age. If we look at a breakdown by gender, we find that in 1970 only one in ten males had not yet married by the time they were thirty-five; for women, the figure was one out of sixteen! The norm of marriages appears to have been very strong in 1970.

Let us compare that year with the year 2000, when about one out of four people had never married by their thirty-fifth birthday. For men it is almost one out of three, and for women it is a little over one out of five. While some may view thirty years as an eternity, it is one generation, and there have been major changes in singlehood in that relatively short period. Let us next explore why these changes have occurred.

Although it is difficult to assess which factors are the most important in influencing any major social change, I believe in this case the one factor that may have been more important than any other is **education**. During the early 1960s the United States experienced a revolution in education. This revolution resulted in the largest number of young people ever to enter institutions of higher learning. Going to college had been something of a rarity in the past. Only members of the upper classes, and a few highly qualified high school students, would continue their education past high school.

Beginning in the early 1960s, this changed. There was a dramatic upswing in college enrollment due to the economic expansion of the 1950s and the increasing ability of larger numbers of families to go without the labor of their children. More and more families could afford to send their children to college. Simultaneously, the economy was changing in a way that demanded a more highly educated workforce. There was a convergence of, on the one hand, the resources that allowed families to send their children to college, and the growing rewards, in terms of careers, at the end of the process. In addition, private colleges and universities expanded their resources to meet the growing demand. There was an increase in state spending on public educational institutions, and state colleges expanded as well. During this period local community colleges developed and grew.

One practical effect of this revolution on singlehood was the fact that most college students do not marry while they are still in college. These students attended college for four or more years, and this extended, almost in a mechanical way, the period of time they remained single. Instead of marrying at eighteen, which a number of people did during the 1950s, these young people were now in college with no thought of getting married.

Education also influenced these young people in an ideological sense. Higher education, for many, opened up a world of possibilities. Higher education created more options. One did not have to follow in the footsteps of one's parents. There were a variety of subjects to study, a variety of areas in which one could major, and a variety of potential career paths. There appeared to be less need to "rush" into marriage. There were other things to do. For many of these students, marriage was something they would like to do, eventually, but not right away.

A second factor that influences the higher rates of singles today is related to increases in educational attainment. This is the nature of the **modern economic system.** The United States economy is largely made up of major corporations. These corporations are both national and international in their business operations. Now let us see how this might affect people remaining single in a hypothetical situation. You are a recent college graduate. You have gone on a number of interviews and are accepted into the management-training program for the Egelman Corporation.

Your training begins in New York City, where you remain for six months. You have successfully completed this program, and I, as president, decide to place you in our office in Seattle, Washington. You spend one year in Seattle, and excel in your work there. I hear about your good work and decide to offer you a promotion, but I need you in our office in Houston, Texas. This process continues for a number of years as you develop a successful career path. Note that intrinsic in this career path is migration.

How can one possibly develop and sustain intimate relationships in this context? Understand that, as you go through these experiences, others are doing the same. The nice person you meet at a party in New York City as you begin your career is on a similar path. As you are asked to leave for Seattle, he or she may be asked by his or her company to move to Atlanta, Georgia! While this is a hypothetical case, it is not far from reality. Many college graduates, perhaps a number of you reading this chapter, will be faced with a similar situation. In some ways the nature of modern postindustrial society may be antithetical to the development of long-term intimate relationships.

An underlying factor connected to both education and the modern work environment is the changing role of women. In the educational revolution discussed earlier, a major subscript of the revolution was the addition of female students to the college environment. While education was limited to a select few in the past, it was especially limited to even fewer women. College classrooms were predominantly white and male. The 1960s changed that. For the first time in U.S. history, large numbers of females entered and graduated from college. This, in turn, led to a large infusion of females into the U.S. workforce.

Both of these changes affect the role of women. Traditionally, and this is discussed throughout this book, a woman's identity was tied to a male, either her father and/or her husband. Today, because of education and the changing labor market, women establish an identity apart from that of any male. If a woman's boyfriend or husband has to move to Seattle, her decision may no longer be an automatic, "Of course I'll move with you to Seattle." Today, she may have wonderful opportunities in Phoenix, or Boston, or some place other than Seattle. Her motivation to be connected to a male for her economic or psychological well-being is not nearly as great as it was in the past. She, too, may find herself in the migratory pattern discussed previously.

A fourth factor that may help account for the growing number of singles is what may be referred to as **backlash.** Specifically, *backlash* refers to reactions to the increase in divorce over the past generation. Almost everyone knows someone who has gone through a divorce, and many young people are concerned with the possibility of divorce. This may sound overly simplistic, but one way to avoid going through divorce is not to get married. While it is not certain that this is the most important factor in singlehood, it is, I believe, a sometimes subtle influence on marital behavior. Sometimes one hears about young people being afraid of intimacy. It may be more accurate to talk about young people being afraid of the result of intimacy gone sour.

A last social factor that influences the rise in singlehood is **social momentum.** The rise in the number of singles is similar to a **social movement.** Social movements are organized efforts to achieve some end. Social momentum is not an organized effort but the results may be the same: a change in society. Rather than being an organized effort, social momentum involves thousands or tens of thousands of people making similar types of decisions. In this case, large numbers of people in their twenties and thirties decided not to get married, at least not to get married at that stage of their life. When this occurs what had been seen as unusual or atypical behavior becomes more usual and more acceptable. In a sense what was "abnormal" becomes "normal."

As an illustration of social momentum, imagine that it is 1955 and you are at your cousin's wedding. You are twenty-nine years old and unmarried. Your Aunt Sarah comes over to you and you can guess what's coming. She says to you in that unmistakable tone, "Well, when will I dance at *your* wedding?" Your own mother hides her face in shame because you are not yet married. Let us now jump ahead to the year 2002. Aunt Sarah may not be so bold in her approach. Why is that the case? It is because her own twenty-nine-year-old child is not yet married. This is social momentum! As more people participate in a particular social pattern, it becomes more acceptable.

Related to this is another factor, a kind of offshoot of social momentum. As more people remain single, there is a greater chance for the development of singles **support networks.** Singles may cluster with other singles and form quasi-family units. If someone gets sick, or if someone simply wants company, there are individuals around to fulfill that function. This is not to suggest that, if one is single, they will not have friends who are married. But married individuals may have issues with their spouse, in-laws, and, possibly, their children. Sometimes the interest of married couples and singles are different. Singles social networks can thus become **fictive family units** fulfilling some of the functions ordinarily thought of as being performed by families.

An additional demographic factor that may influence the proportion of singles in a society is what is called the **marriage squeeze.** In order for everyone to get married, there needs to be an approximately equal number of males and females. The number of males to females is called the **sex ratio.** More specifically, the sex ratio is the number of males available for every one hundred females. For example, in the sixty-five and over population, the sex ratio is approximately sixty-four. This means that, for every one hundred females sixty-five and over, there are sixty-four males sixty-five and over.

Under certain circumstances, and for certain selected groups, there may be atypical sex ratios. For example, in periods of war, when men are the sole group of soldiers, there tend to be fewer marriages due to a distorted sex ratio in the civilian population. Also, the loss of life in a war can affect marriage rates in the post-war period. Another example would be African American women today. Highly educated African American women tend to have lower marriage rates than other women due to the fact that there are greater numbers of highly educated females than there are males in this particular group. In addition, interracial marriage is not widespread among African Americans so they tend not to find partners outside of their group (see Chapter 2).

All these factors appear to indicate that singlehood is a viable option for growing numbers of people. Interestingly, large numbers of people in their twenties and thirties say they would like to eventually marry. Whether they will or not is difficult to predict. The United States has always been a marrying society. Running counter to this is the actual behavior of millions of people. There is a type of sociological axiom that says that the longer one stays in a certain lifestyle the more likely it is the person will remain in that lifestyle. As people delay or defer getting married, the greater the likelihood they will not get married. It will be interesting to see twenty years from now what has happened to the current generation of singles.

In the next section, you will have the opportunity to examine changes in the singles population over time, with respect to differences by gender, and racial/ethnic category.

Analysis

TABLE 8.1   *Never-Married People 15 Years and over (in one thousands): 2000*

Age	Total No.	Total Never Married	Percent
	213,773	60,016	
15–19	20,102	19,541	
20–24	18,440	14,430	
25–29	18,269	8,252	
30–34	19,519	5,071	
35–44	44,804	6,932	
45–54	36,633	3,303	
55–64	23,388	1,218	
65 and over	32,620	1,270	

Source: U.S. Census Bureau, *American Families and Living Arrangements,* June 2001, pp. 20–537.

1. First, examine the changes in the proportion of people remaining single in American society. Table 8.1 presents data on never-married people by age. Calculate the percentage of people never married for the year 2000 and put your answers in the table.

2. What general statements can you make about the distribution of never-married people by age?

TABLE 8.2   *Never-Married People 15 Years and over: 1970 and 2000*

Age	1970	2000	Difference
Total	24.9		
15–19	93.9		
20–24	44.5		
25–29	14.7		
30–34	7.8		
35–44	5.9		
45–54	6.1		
55–64	7.2		
65 and over	7.6		

Source: U.S. Census Bureau, *American Families and Living Arrangements,* June 2001, pp. 20–537.

3. How do these data compare to singles in the past? Table 8.2 presents data on the percentage never married for 1970, place the percentages you calculated for 2000 in the allotted space in the table and calculate the difference for each age category and put your answers in the table.

4. Which three age categories show the largest difference?

5. How does the pattern in 1970 compare to the pattern you found in 2000?

6. What factors contribute to the differences you discovered?

TABLE 8.3 *Never-Married People 15 Years and over by Sex: 2000*

Age	Males			Females		
	Total No.	Single	Percent	Total No.	Single	Percent
Total	103,113	32,253		110,660	27,763	
15–19	10,295	10,140		9,807	9,401	
20–24	9,208	7,710		9,232	6,720	
25–29	8,943	4,625		9,326	3,627	
30–34	9,622	2,899		9,897	2,172	
35–44	22,134	3,981		22,670	2,951	
45–54	17,891	1,697		18,742	1,606	
55–64	11,137	612		12,252	606	
65 and over	13,885	590		18,735	680	

Source: U.S. Census Bureau, *American Families and Living Arrangements,* June 2001, pp. 20–537.

7. Are men more likely to remain single than women are? Table 8.3 presents data on never-married people by sex. Calculate the percentage of never-married for males and females and put your answers in the table.

8. What comparisons may be made in the pattern of never-married people for males and females?

9. What might account for the differences you found in the data?

TABLE 8.4   *Never-Married People 15 Years and over by Sex: 1970 and 2000*

	Males			Females		
Age	1970	2000	Difference	1970	2000	Difference
Total	28.1			22.1		
15–19	97.4			90.3		
20–24	54.7			35.8		
25–29	19.1			10.5		
30–34	9.4			6.2		
35–44	6.7			5.2		
45–54	7.5			4.9		
55–64	7.8			6.8		
65 and over	7.5			7.7		

Source: U.S. Census Bureau, *American Families and Living Arrangements,* June 2001, pp. 20–537.

10. Now examine how the patterns for 2000 compare to the pattern in the year 1970. Place the percentages you found in Table 8.3 in the appropriate space in Table 8.4, and calculate the differences for both males and females.

11. What age categories have the largest differences for males?

12. What age categories have the largest differences for females?

13. In general, how would you characterize the differences you found in the never-married data for the years 1970 and 2000?

TABLE 8.5   *Percentage of Never-Married People by Race and Hispanic Origin: 1980 to 1999*

Race and Origin	1980	1990	1999
White	18.9	20.3	21.4
Black	30.5	35.1	39.2
Hispanic	24.1	27.2	29.0

Source: U.S. Census, *Statistical Abstract of the United States: 2000,* Table 53.

14. As a last factor, examine how the role of race/ethnicity may play in patterns of singlehood. Table 8.5 presents data on the percentages of never-married by year. What similarities appear for all three groups?

15. What differences appear for all three groups?

16. What factors might explain the differences?

17. Given the data you have examined in this chapter, what projections can you make about the future of singlehood in the United States?

Selected Bibliography and Suggested Readings _____

Anderson, C., Stewart, Susan, & Dimidjian, Sona. (1994). *Flying solo: Single women in midlife.* New York: Norton.

Edwards, Tamala. (2000, August 29). Flying Solo. *Time,* 47–53.

Gordon, T. (1994). *Single women: On the margins?* New York: New York University Press.

Landale, D., & Tolnay, S. (1991). Group differences in economic opportunity and the timing of marriage. *American Sociological Review 56,* 33–45.

Nakosteen, R., & Zimmer, M. (1997). Men, money, and marriage: Are high earners more prone than low earners to marry? *Social Science Quarterly 78,* 66–82.

Paul, Pamela. (2002). *Starter marriage and the future of matrimony.* New York: Random House.

Simenauer, J., & Carroll, D. (1982). *Singles: The new Americans.* New York: Simon and Schuster.

South, Scott. (1993). Racial and ethnic differences in the desire to marry. *Journal of Marriage and the Family 55,* 357–370.

Stein, Peter. (Ed.). (1981). *Single life: Unmarried adults in social context.* New York: St. Martin's Press.

Taylor, R., Jackson, James, & Chatters, Linda. (Eds.). (1997). *Family life in black America.* Thousand Oaks, CA: Sage.

ıcker, Belinda, & Mitchell-Kernan, Claudia. (Eds.). (1995). *The decline in marriage among African Americans.* New York: Russell Sage.

9

Cohabitation: A Modern Variation of Marriage?

"Living together," "shacking up," "nonmarital cohabitation," "unmarried partners," "persons of opposite sex sharing living quarters" are all of the ways describing couples who live together and share an intimate lifestyle without being married.

In the past, depending on the era, heterosexuals who lived together without being married were often seen as living in sin, as bohemians, beatniks, radicals, communists, or deviants. In the last twenty years the number of individuals who choose to live this way has more than doubled, going from 3.2 million in 1980 to 7.6 million in the year 2000. While estimates vary, researchers estimate that somewhere between one-third and one-half of all married couples lived together prior to getting married. What accounts for this change in the number of heterosexuals living together out of wedlock? We can divide the factors into two categories: **the sociological** and **individual.** Let us examine the larger, sociological factors first.

One major factor that has contributed to the number of heterosexuals living in intimate relations outside of wedlock is the changes that have occurred with respect to **sexual norms.** Historically, the United States has been seen a **Puritan society**, with stringent rules regarding sexual behavior. Sex was only supposed to take place within marriage, between people of different sexes. Ironically, evidence suggests that even the Puritans of the seventeenth century engaged in premarital sex. The difference was that many of these couples were engaged and did marry prior to the actual birth of their children. Other evidence suggests that this may have been a pattern that has existed throughout American history.

Today, values regarding sexual behavior have changed. While it is difficult to pinpoint the exact time when changes began to occur, there is little question that attitudes are substantially different today compared to the past. Some suggest that the initial movement for "sexual liberation" occurred at the turn of the century with the growth of the women's suffrage movement. Others suggest that it was the "Roaring 20s," with the emergence of nightlife and popular entertainment. Still others argue for the World War II period with its increasing numbers of women in the workforce. Still others suggest the "hippie movement" of the 1960s.

What is the nature of this change? The research evidence appears to make a strong argument that more and more people engage in sexual relations without being married. Also, the research indicates that young people engage in sexual behavior at earlier ages than in the past. Sexual messages, both implicit and explicit, are strewn across the various mass media. Popular songs, movies, and even daytime and evening television shows present clear sexual messages. This author can clearly remember growing up in the 1950s, when television shows rarely, if ever, showed even married couples in the bedroom. And, if they were in the bedroom, the husband and wife could not be shown sitting on the bed together! Today, television shows are much more explicit in their presentation of adult sexual relations.

These shows reflect the shift in attitudes that have occurred since World War II. Today, many people view sex as the prerogative of the adult. There appears to be a wide range of values regarding sexual behavior. Some feel that sex is part of adult entertainment and any two consenting adults at any time may wish to engage in sexual relations. This is seen as their right. Perhaps more common is the belief that sex is part of adult relationships, and any two adults who are in the process of developing an intimate relationship will also engage in sexual interaction. The change in attitude may be best summed up by saying that, in the past, marriage was the time one was permitted to engage in sexual behavior, and today falling in love is the time to engage in sexual behavior.

Related to the changes in sexual attitudes and behavior is the development of modern forms of **contraception.** Contraception use goes back to ancient times. Even the ancient Egyptians made use of artificial forms of contraception, and there have always been "natural" forms of contraception. For contraception to be effective, two elements must be present. First, modern technology leads to the production of safe and effective means of contraception. However, for this technology to make an impact a second element must also be present: a value system that allows for the use of the technology.

Contraception is available in most countries of the world but its use is widely varied (see Chapter 1). What makes for this variation in use are the value systems in the countries. Some traditional value systems are very resistant to the use of contraception while more modern value systems appear to see contraceptive use as normal and acceptable. In the United

States, some groups are opposed to the use of this technology, but most Americans do use some form of modern contraceptive technology. Contraceptive use is related to cohabitation insofar as a cohabiting couple may not wish to have children, so their intimate relations can proceed without fertility issues arising.

A third sociological factor that may have influenced patterns of cohabitation is the development of **urban society. Urbanization** is the process whereby large numbers of people come to live in cities. **Urbanism** is the cultural values typically associated with urban life. These include diversity, tolerance, and openness to new ideas. The United States is largely an urban society. Most Americans live in cities or their suburbs. Largely due to the mass media, urbanism exists throughout much of the country regardless of whether the area is a city, suburb, or even a rural area. Urbanism has what one might term a macrosociological effect on cohabitation. Values associated with urbanism increase the potential for new and innovative lifestyles, including cohabitation.

A fourth factor is that of **education.** Here, however, there does appear to be an ironic twist. On the one hand higher education is usually associated with many of the values associated with urbanism: diversity, tolerance, and openness to new ideas. So as more people achieve higher education, one may expect that greater numbers of these highly educated people would be more likely to live together out of wedlock. What is ironic about this relationship is that some data indicate that people with less education are more likely to cohabit than more highly educated people. The data are still open to interpretation and you will have the opportunity to grapple with this question when you analyze the data in Table 8.3 later in this chapter. It may be the case that cohabitation has become such a widespread phenomenon that it now cuts across differences in levels of educational attainment.

A last sociological factor to be discussed is **divorce.** Divorce affects cohabitation in two distinct ways. First, there is a demographic factor. Divorced people become eligible to marry again. They create a pool of potential partners. Because they were divorced, some number of them may not wish to "rush into" another marriage. Cohabitation may be a viable alternative for those divorced people seeking intimate relations without the legal ramifications of marriage.

A second factor attributable to divorce is a **fear of marriage,** but this might be more accurately described as a **fear of divorce.** With divorce so widespread in our society, there are few, if any, people who do not have some close relative or friend who has gone through a divorce, and they witness all the stresses and strains connected with the divorce process (see Chapter 6). They have no desire to have this type of experience, and cohabitation for them may be a way of avoiding divorce.

Having examined some of the larger sociological factors let us next turn to some **individual factors** that contribute to the formation of cohabiting relationships. Perhaps the most basic individual motivation is the desire for intimacy. Most people seem to need intimate relations. Cohabitation, by definition, implies intimacy. The extent of intimacy in cohabiting relationships may of course vary. Along with the general search for intimacy, cohabitation provides for a steady sexual partner. It is also usually assumed that cohabiting relationships will involve less game playing than traditional dating relationships. Sharing a household means one does not have to wait for the phone call asking for a date. Some cohabitors see living together as a relatively free, fun-loving type of relationship. It avoids the strings of marriage while providing for a variety of the benefits. At some level this type of relationship may also serve as a source of security to those involved, as a way of avoiding loneliness. It also allows for personal growth that comes with experiencing intimate relationships. Although certainly not an exhaustive list, this may a serve as a kind of typology of individual motivations for cohabitation.

Prior to moving on to the analysis section, some additional observations may be made. First, the **legal rights of cohabitants** are not clearly laid out in the law. Remember that all family law is state law so that there are fifty sets of laws regarding family life. The same holds true for cohabitants. There is no federal standard and any set of laws has been created by the particular state. The general observation experts make is that cohabitants have relatively few rights in legal matters. Issues of inheritance or property rights are not clearly defined, as they tend to be with marriage.

There is a great deal of variation in the length of time cohabitants spend in any one cohabiting relationship, but the average length of time is approximately eighteen months. At least when compared to marriages, these relationships are rather short-lived. Even when compared to couples who get divorced, this holds true. The median number of years a divorced couple remains married is approximately seven years. This means that 50 percent of all divorced couples divorce within the first seven years of marriage, and 50 percent of all divorced couples divorce after seven years of marriage.

As with divorce, the presence of children will complicate the cohabiting relationship. Since 1980 the number of children involved in this type of household has increased almost fourfold. Interestingly, the presence of children seems to influence cohabiting relationships. If children are present, such relationships tend to last for longer periods of time. Of course, and again as with divorce, the presence of children raises questions of stepparenting and the difficulties this type of relationship may face.

Does cohabiting affect the success of later marriages? The evidence indicates there may be little if any impact. One might think that cohabitors have lower divorce rates than noncohabitors, but it is just the reverse. Cohabitors are even more likely to divorce than noncohabitors. The relationship between cohabiting and divorce, however, may be a spurious one. A **spurious relationship** is when researchers believe there is a relationship between two variables, when, in fact, there is a third variable that is affecting both variables independently. In this discussion there is a belief that cohabiting (variable A) influences divorce (variable B), but there is another possibility. Heterosexuals with liberal attitudes (variable C) will be more likely to cohabit than those with conservative or traditional attitudes. Heterosexuals with liberal attitudes may also be more likely to divorce if they are in an unhappy marriage. Thus, it may be that liberal attitudes are the key factor in explaining both divorce and cohabiting patterns.

A last question that may be raised is what is the general meaning of cohabitation? What will its impact be on family structure and dynamics? There appears to be two possible interpretations. First, cohabitation will become a step toward marriage. It may be seen as a new approach to traditional dating. Second, cohabitation will become an alternative to marriage whereby large numbers of cohabitants never marry and come to see cohabitation as the permanent or quasi-permanent relationship in their lives. It may be that both are true. For some couples it is a first step toward marriage. For others, it is an alternative to marriage. Cohabitation has added to the diversity of family life in both the United States and in other parts of the world.

Now let's examine some of the data related to this lifestyle by analyzing some of the key characteristics of cohabitants and comparing them to those of married couples.

Analysis

TABLE 9.1 *Married and Unmarried Couples: 1980–2000 (in millions)*

| Year | Married Couples | | Unmarried Couples | |
	Number	% Change	Number	% Change
1980	52.3	NA	1.6	NA
1990	56.3		2.9	
2000	56.5		3.8	

Source: U.S. Census Bureau, *Statistical Abstract of the United States: 2000,* Tables 37, 53; *America's Families and Living Arrangements 2000,* June 2001, pp. 20–537.

1. First, examine the recent growth rate for unmarried couples, and compare it to the growth rate of married couples. Table 9.1 presents data on the number of married couples and the number of unmarried couples. Calculate the percentage increase in growth rate for married and unmarried couples between 1980 and 1990 and between 1990 and 2000 and put your answers in the table.

2. Which category has experienced the largest percentage increase?

3. Another way of comparing these two categories is to calculate a ratio. A ratio is one number that compares two different categories. In order to calculate the ratio married couples to unmarried couples, divide the number of married couples by the number of unmarried couples. For example, in 1980 the ratio would be 52.3/1.6. The result is 32.69. You may round this to 33. This number could be interpreted as follows: for every 33 married couples there was one unmarried couple. Now calculate the ratio for 1990. _____

4. Calculate the ratio for 2000. _____

5. What pattern emerges from your calculations?

TABLE 9.2 *Age Distribution for Married and Unmarried Couples (in thousands): 2000*

	Married Couples				Unmarried Couples			
Age	Males	Percent	Females	Percent	Males	Percent	Females	Percent
Total	56,497		56,497		3,822		3,822	
15–24	1,321		2,386		597		937	
25–34	9,296		10,964		1,413		1,269	
35 and over	45,881		43,146		1,811		1,616	

Source: U.S. Census Bureau, *America's Families and Living Arrangements 2000,* June 2001, pp. 20–537.

6. Next, examine some of the characteristics of unmarried couples and compare these to the characteristics of married couples. Table 9.2 presents data on age and marital status for males and females. Calculate the percentage distribution by age and sex in the spaces allotted in the table.

7. Compare the patterns you found for the two groups.

TABLE 9.3 *Educational Attainment for Married and Unmarried Couples (in thousands): 2000*

Age	Married Couples				Unmarried Couples			
	Males	Percent	Females	Percent	Males	Percent	Females	Percent
Total	56,497		56,497		3,822		3,822	
Less than high school	8,314		7,160		683		599	
High school graduate	17,506		19,950		1,441		1,357	
Some college	14,002		14,968		996		1,223	
College graduate	16,674		14,419		702		643	

Source: U.S. Census Bureau, *America's Families and Living Arrangements 2000,* June 2001, pp. 20–537.

8. How does education affect living arrangements? Table 9.3 compares the level of educational attainment and living arrangements. As you did in Table 9.2, calculate the percentage distribution by education for Table 9.3 and put your answers in the table.

9. Compare the two patterns you found.

TABLE 9.4 *Selected Characteristics of Married and Unmarried Couples: 2000*

Characteristics	Married Couples	Unmarried Couples
Age Difference		
Male 6 or more years older than female	19.6	24.7
Female 6 or more years older than male	3.3	9.1
Race/Ethnic Difference		
Interracial couples	1.9	4.3
Hispanic/non-Hispanic couples	3.1	5.8

Source: U.S. Census Bureau, *America's Families and Living Arrangements 2000,* June 2001, pp. 20–537.

10. Compare the age differences between married and unmarried couples in Table 9.4.

11. Compare the racial and ethnic differences between married and un-married couples in Table 9.4.

12. Why do you think these differences appear in the data?

TABLE 9.5 *Unmarried-Couple Households by Presence of Children under 15 Years Old: 1978–2000*

Year	Total No. Households	With Children[1]	Percent
1980	1,587	431	
1990	2,856	891	
2000	3,822	1,563	

[1] For the year 2000, children are under 18 years of age.

Source: U.S. Census Bureau, *America's Families and Living Arrangements 2000,* June 2001; Un-married-Couple households, by Presence of Children: 1960 to Present, January 7, 1999 www.census.gov/population/socdemo/ms-la/tabad-2.txt

13. In discussions of cohabitation, the issue of children often emerges. Table 9.5 indicates the number of children present in unmarried-couple households over time. Calculate the percentage of children present in such households for the time period covered in the table and put your answers in the space provided.

14. What pattern did you find in the data?

15. Calculate the percentage increase in total number of households from 1980 to 2000.

16. Calculate the percentage of these households with children for the years 1980 and 2000.

17. Which category grew faster?

18. Why do you believe this pattern emerges from the data?

19. What issues related to parenting may arise because of this pattern?

20. Given the data you have analyzed in this chapter, what implications could this have for your understanding of the family?

Selected Bibliography and Suggested Readings _____

Benokraitis, Nijole. (2002). *Marriages and families: Changes, choices, and constraints* (4th ed.). Upper Saddle River, NJ: Prentice-Hall. (See pp. 203–209.)

Blackwell, Debra, & Lichter, Daniel. (2000). "Mate selection among married and cohabiting couples." *Journal of Family Issues 21,* 275–302.

Bumpus, L., & Lu, H. (2000). "Trends in cohabitation and implications for children's family contexts in the United States." *Population Studies 54,* 29–41.

Bumpass, L., & Sweet, J. (1991). "The role of cohabitation in declining rates of marriage." *Journal of Marriage and the Family 53,* 913–927.

Buunk, Bram, & van Driel, Barry. (1989). *Variant lifestyles and relationships.* Newbury Park, CA: Sage.

Cox, Frank. (2002). *Human intimacy: Marriage, the family, and its meaning* (9th ed.). Belmont, CA: Wadsworth. (See pp. 174–182.)

Oppenheimer, V. (1994). "Women's rising employment and the future of family in industrial societies." *Population and Development Review 20,* 293–342.

Reigot, B., & Spina, R. (1996). *Beyond the traditional family: Voices of diversity.* New York: Springer.

Smock, P. (2000). Cohabitation in the United States: An appraisal of research themes, findings, and implications. *Annual Review of Sociology 26,* 1–20.

10

Working Women: Why Aren't They in the Kitchen?

Sociologists often speak of families, in the United States and elsewhere, as having two distinct sets of functions. One set of functions is called **instrumental functions.** These functions include the practical elements of family life: protection, and supplying food, clothing, and shelter. **Expressive functions** include the emotional or nurturing elements of family life including such activities as offering emotional support, using someone's shoulder to cry on, and, especially, trying to meet the emotional needs of children. Traditionally, instrumental functions were seen as the venue for a male's activity in the family while expressive functions were seen as the domain for the females in the family.

This view of functional responsibilities is what may be termed **ideal types.** Ideal types reflect what researchers believe to be the case in real culture. The husband as husband/breadwinner and the wife as wife/homemaker are examples of the ideal type. Such ideal types almost always ignore the diversity that really exists in any society. In this chapter we will explore the ideal type of the woman as wife/homemaker.

There is a widespread belief that in the past women did not work. Even a superficial examination of this idea would immediately reveal that this image is false. Women have always worked. In many cultures, and throughout much of history, their work was done probably within the family setting. Daughters helped their mothers and fathers do the agricultural work that had to be done for the family's survival. I specify agricultural work because, throughout most of human history, most people worked in agriculture.

As the woman matured she would marry and then do the same type of work with her husband. Women were often seen as relatively powerless partners who took orders from their husbands. In these **patriarchal** societies men were seen as having all the power. Closer inspection suggests something else. In many of these societies, women had what might be termed **hidden power.** Many times it was actually the wife who ran the family business. She was the one who brought the produce to the market, negotiated prices with the customers, and then decided how the money would be spent. She was the one who decided how much allowance she gave her husband.

Today there has been a shift in female work patterns. This shift is not from not working to working; rather, it involves what kind of work and with whom. What some see as the revolution of female work really involves the emergence of independent female work. Independent, in this case, means independent from a male family member. Women today develop their own career paths, separate and apart from any male relative. The remainder of this chapter will examine some of the causes for this trend, and how this trend may affect various aspects of family life. First, I will discuss the importance of work.

Work, perhaps most importantly, supplies one with the means to survive financially. When people think of "good jobs" they think of jobs that are high paying. Obviously such jobs create access to all types of material rewards including housing, clothing, and even vacations.

In addition to these material rewards, there are a number of social and psychological rewards. In the United States personal identity is often tied to the work one does. When one is introduced to a stranger one of the first questions asked is: "What do you do?" Occupation, in a sociological sense, places people in a particular **status position.** By knowing someone's occupation we can place them in some social ranking system. Not only do strangers do this, but we do this to ourselves as well. One's sense of self, the degree of self-pride one has, and even one's sense of personal dignity is very much influenced by what we have achieved, and this definition of achievement is often tied to what we have achieved in the workplace.

The workplace also provides for social interaction. Meeting at the water cooler, having luncheon meetings, and the everyday camaraderie that develops between co-workers allows for a variety of social interactions. For example, while raising a child may be very rewarding, for some people being with a one-year-old all day long may deprive the person of the stimulation ordinarily available from adult interaction.

More specifically, this desire for adult interaction is one of the causes for the increase in women working. Raising a child may have its own rewards, and certainly there are still large numbers of mothers who do not work, but many women do not find this activity rewarding enough to leave the work environment. As an aside, one should try avoiding any stereotypic thinking about mothers who stay home and those that return to work. Women who stay home are not lazy, and women who go out to work are not neglectful of their children. Women make different choices based on their own needs and the needs of their family. The increased numbers of working women indicate that the choices women have are more diverse today than they were in the past.

A second factor that has contributed to increasing numbers of women working is changes in levels of **educational attainment.** As noted throughout this book, one of the major social changes in the United States since World War II has been the increase in the number of women completing high school and then going on and achieving a college degree. Women, as do men, invest at least four years of their life, and a relatively large sum of money, to complete their education. With a college degree in hand, many of the women then want to enjoy the fruits of their educational investment. That is, they wish to engage in stimulating and rewarding work.

Having completed college, women enter **career paths.** While there is evidence that there is gender discrimination is some sectors of the economy, there is little question that there are greater opportunities for women today compared to the past. The **opportunity structure** has changed. In the past young women would go into nursing, but certainly not become doctors, at least in any large numbers. So, too, women might become bookkeepers but not accountants. Today, approximately 50 percent of all entrants to medical school are female, and over 50 percent of all accountants are now female.

What accounts for this shift in the changing nature of women's aspirations? In the past there existed a gender-based occupational system. Little girls were told they could be nurses, and they would make believe they were nurses in their childish play. Today, more and more parents may motivate little girls to pretend they are doctors. Another motivation to aspire to higher level occupations and a greater variety of occupations is that many young girls today see their mothers going out to work.

A last factor that serves as a motivation to go out to work is money. Many women work because they have to. They may be single, and living on their own. They may be single parents because either they never married or they are divorced. They may be married but their income is essential for the family's well-being; or, they may wish to maintain a certain type of lifestyle associated with two-income families. The motivations to work vary by social class. Lower-class and working-class women work because of the financial necessity. Middle- and upper-class women may work either to maintain the lifestyle to which they are accustomed or to achieve a higher level of economic success.

Regardless of the kind of work women engage in, there does appear to be substantial differences in male and female earnings. This may be due to a number of factors. Women may enter lower-status, and lower-paying, positions. Another factor is that large numbers of women have entered the workforce in r tively recent times, so many of these women may have less seniority ; d fewer years in their chosen occupation. Also, women do take some tin off for childbearing and childbearing responsibilities. This also may res in lower seniority. A last factor may be **institutional discrimination** which is much more difficult to measure. Institutional discrimination discrimination that is embedded in society. It is difficult to measure be use it results from the typical workings of society. For example, if a po ion in the workforce has a height requirement, and if women, on averag re not as tall as men are, then women would be less likely to get the p ition. The height requirement is not a conscious attempt to eliminate vomen from consideration, but the result is women will not have the ame opportunity as men to be hired for that position. Circumstantial idence and anecdotal reports suggest that some degree of discrimina on still exists in the labor market. You will have the opportunity to eval te some of these data in the analysis section.

V iile we have focused on women's motivations to work, there is also a nee to talk a little bit about changing male perceptions regarding wom 's work. Some men still take the traditional view that women's activiti should be focused on the home as wife/mother. It is inconceivable, how ver, that such changes could have taken place without some changes in t e male perspective. Fathers, boyfriends, husbands, and perhaps even sor play some role in the changes that have occurred. For most men, it ha become an almost taken-for-granted idea that the women in their lives w be actively engaged in their own career, so the attitudinal shift we have w nessed is not just on the part of females. Males, too, have had to change t eir perceptions and expectations.

What are some of the possible effects of this changing trend on family fe? First, what impact will this have on dating and marriage? Dating may ecome more problematic as both men and women pursue careers. As noted in Chapter 8, career mobility often involves geographic mobility. In order to make moves within a company you often have to move where the company sends you. If men and women are both traveling around the country seeking career opportunities it is more difficult to engage in long-term intimate relationships. Marriage faces the same problem. How do you get to the point of deciding to marry if the person you met six months ago in New York City now works in Miami and you now work in Chicago (see Chapter 2)?

On the other hand, it is possible that working women may become more attractive in the mate selection process. In the past one of the definitions of a "good catch" for women wishing to marry was that the man made a "good living." Now we may see a reversal of sorts, with men seeking out women who make a good living. The woman's earnings or potential for earnings may make her a good "catch." Evidence does suggest that college-educated women who enter a career path are somewhat less likely to marry than other women. This may be especially true for the most educated women who have entered the highest status career paths. Traditionally, there is an assumption that the husband will make more money than the wife. If it holds true then the potential pool of eligible partners for this particular group of women may be quite small.

Once marriage has taken place, what then of the marital relationship? As with dating there may be pros and cons. The fact that both the husband and wife work may mean that each is more preoccupied with his or her work than with the marital relationship. The demands of work may mean that each comes home either emotionally and/or physically exhausted. One or both may have difficulty juggling the demands of work and the elements that go into making for a successful marriage. On the other hand, data suggest that one good indicator of successful marriages is that each party to the marriage has a positive self-image. People who are happy with themselves are much more likely to create happy marriages. In this instance, the couple may be able to exchange stories about their experiences at work. To some degree each partner may find the other more interesting to be with. The couple may share experiences and develop a stronger empathetic relationship.

Fertility rates also appear to be influenced by female work patterns. There appears to be a universal relationship between fertility and women's education (see Chapter 3). Regardless of the society, there is a general pattern of higher educated women having fewer children. If we add to this the dedication some women have to their careers then it is not surprising to find lower fertility among working women.

Regardless of the number of children, with working women there is always the issue of child care. Who watches the children while the mother is working? One answer might be the father, if the father is present, but the father may be working as well. Some parents try to juggle their work time so that each can spend time with the child. This assumes that whomever they work for will be flexible in deciding work schedules. The parents may rely on other family members, but that is not always practical because they may work or live some distance away.

The parents may seek out child-care facilities. There have been some scandals involving child-care centers, so some parents may be afraid to use these facilities. If fear is not the issue, cost may be a factor. Especially for poorer families, child care may be too costly for them. Some families make use of informal child care—older women who live in the neighborhood and are willing to take children into their own homes or use the child's home. The problem in this instance is that these women are not licensed and, although many of them may make excellent child-care providers, there is certainly no guarantee as to their competence.

Clearly, patterns of labor force participation have affected family systems. The analysis section will give you the opportunity to examine some of the changes in labor force participation trends, and to also examine gender differences in earnings.

Analysis

TABLE 10.1 *Employed People in the Civilian Population by Sex and Year (in thousands): 1970–2001*

	Male		Female	
Year	Number	Percentage Change	Number	Percentage Change
1970	48,990		29,668	
1990	65,104		53,689	
2001	71,926		63,006	

Source: U.S. Census Bureau, *Statistical Abstract of the United States, 2000,* Table 645; U.S. Department of Labor, Bureau of Labor Statistics, *Household Data: Historical,* Table 2A; www.stats.bls.gov/web/empsit.supp.toc.html#nseason

1. First, examine changes in the number of women and men who are working. Table 10.1 presents data on people employed in the civilian population. Calculate the percentage change of employed persons in the space allotted in the table. You may use the following formula to calculate percent change:

$$\frac{1990 - 1970}{1970} \times 100 = \text{Percentage Change}$$

2. Which gender category has experienced the greatest percentage change?

3. For which period was the change the greatest?

4. Why do you believe this time period showed the greatest change?

5. Another way to compare the two groups is to create a ratio of male workers to female workers. This is simply done by dividing the number of male workers by the number of female workers. What is the ratio for the year 1970? _____

6. For 1990? _____

7. For 2001? _____

8. What may account for the pattern you have discovered?

TABLE 10.2 *Labor Force Activity of Married Couples (in thousands):*
1986 to 2000

Labor Force Activity	2000		1986	
	Number	*Percent*	*Number*	*Percent*
All married couples	55,311		50,933	
In labor force:				
Husband and wife	31,095		25,428	
Husband only	11,815		14,675	
Wife only	3,301		2,362	
Neither in labor force	9,098		8,468	

Source: U.S. Census Bureau, *Married Couples by Labor Force Status of Spouses: 1986 to Present,*
revised July 26, 2001, www.census.gov/population/socdemo/hh-fam/tabMC-1.txt

9. Next, determine how marriage affects work. Table 10.2 presents data on married couples and who works in those relationships. Calculate the percentage distribution of work patterns for the years indicated and put your answers in the table.

10. What general observations can you make about work patterns for the fifteen-year period covered in the table?

TABLE 10.3 *Labor Force Activity of Married Couples with Children under Six Years of Age (in thousands): 1986 to 2000*

Labor Force Activity	2000		1986	
	Number	Percent	Number	Percent
All married couples	11,393		11,924	
In labor force:				
Husband and wife	6,984		6,271	
Husband only	4,077		5,284	
Wife only	211		155	
Neither in labor force	121		215	

Source: U.S. Census Bureau, Married Couples by Labor Force Status of Spouses: 1986 to Present, last revised July 2001, www.census.gov/population/socdemo/hh-fam/tabMC-1.txt

11. What impact do young children have on work patterns? Table 10.3 presents data on work patterns with the presence of children under the age of six. As with Table 9.2, calculate the percentage distribution of work patterns and put your answers in the table.

12. Describe the differences you find between 1986 and 2000.

13. How do children affect work patterns?

TABLE 10.4 *Median Earnings by Educational Level and Sex: 1991–2001*

	2001			1991		
	Male	Female	Difference	Male	Female	Difference
Less than 9th grade	14,594	8,846		10,319	6,268	
High school graduate	28,343	15,665		21,546	10,818	
Bachelor's degree or higher	54,069	33,842		39,803	23,627	

Source: U.S. Census Bureau, *Educational Attainment: People 25 Years Old and Over by Median Income and Sex: 1991 to 2001,* revised September 30, 2002. www.census.gov/hhes/income/histinc/p16.html

14. A major issue related to women and work is the difference in income between women and men. Examine this issue by comparing median incomes to the level of educational attainment. Median income is the midpoint for all earners. For example, in Table 10.4 the median income for all males in 2001 was $32,494. This means that 50 percent of all males earned more, and 50 percent earned less. Calculate the difference in median income for the educational categories and years indicated in the table and put your answers in the table.

15. For which educational category are the differences the greatest?

16. Why do you think this is the case?

17. How have income differences changed over time?

18. Why has this change occurred?

TABLE 10.5 *Median Weekly Earnings of Full-Time Wage and Salary Workers for Selected Occupations by Sex: 2000*

Occupation	Males	Females	Difference
Registered nurses	890	782	
Elementary school teachers	860	701	
Social workers	637	589	
Cashiers	313	276	
Bookkeepers	539	478	

Source: U.S. Department of Labor, Bureau of Labor Statistics, *Household Data: Annual Averages,* Table 39; ftp://ftp.bls.gov/pub/special.requests/1f/aat39.txt

19. We can approach this analysis of income differences another way. Examine some traditional female occupations and compare the median weekly earnings for men and women who work in those occupations. Table 10.5

presents data on selected occupations. In each case, the number of females employed was at least twice the number of men employed. Calculate the difference in weekly earnings for males and females in these traditionally female occupations and put your answers in the table.

20. What might account for the income differences noted in the table?

21. Based on your analysis of these data, how do women's work experiences compare to those of men?

Selected Bibliography and Suggested Readings

Baxandell, Rosalyn, & Gordon, Linda. (Eds.). (1995). *America's working women: A documentary history, 1600 to the present* (Rev. Ed.). New York: Norton.

Bradley, Harriet. (1989). *Men's work, women's work.* Minneapolis: University of Minnesota Press.

Garey, A. (1999). *Weaving work and motherhood.* Philadelphia: Temple University Press.

Hays, S. (1996). *The cultural contradictions of motherhood.* New Haven: Yale University Press.

Hochschild, Arlie. (1989). *The second shift: Working parents and the revolution at home.* New York: Viking.

Hochschild, Arlie. (1997). *The time bind: When work becomes home and home becomes work.* New York: Holt.

Levine, Suzanne. (2000). *Father courage: What happens when men put family first.* New York: Harcourt.

Moen, P. (1992). *Women's two roles: A contemporary dilemma.* Westport, CT: Auburn House.

O'Reilly, A., & Abbey, S. (Eds.). (2000). *Mothers and daughters: Connection, empowerment, and transformation.* Lanham, MD: Rowman and Littlefield.

Rubin, Lillian. (1994). *Families on the fault line: America's working class speaks about the family, the economy, race, and ethnicity.* New York: HarperCollins.

Yorburg, Betty. (2002). *Family realities: A global view.* Upper Saddle River, NJ: Prentice-Hall.

11

Two-Worker Families

One of the major outcomes of the increase in working women (see Chapter 10) is the impact it has on the nature of family life. More specifically, today we find greater numbers of two-worker families in which both husband and wife are in the labor force. This phenomenon has been referred to in a variety of ways: *dual-worker family, dual-career family,* and *dual-earner family* are among the most common terms. *Dual-career family,* many researchers believe, is inadequate because it suggests that all dual-worker families are in the middle class. That is why some researchers developed the terms *dual-worker* and *dual-earner* family to include those families not in the middle class.

I will use the term *dual-worker family* to represent all families, regardless of class, in which both husband and wife are in the labor force. As the discussion proceeds, mention will be made of social class differences as it becomes relevant. Regardless of the term used, this type of family has become the **modal type** of family in the United States. As of 2000, approximately 54 percent of all families fall into this category. Even if children are present this still holds true. For example, 50 percent of all married couples who have a child under the age of one are dual-worker families. For married couples with children under the age of five, the percentage increases to almost 57 percent.

This chapter will focus on seven issues related to dual-worker families: the marital issue, childrearing issue, homemaker issue, workplace issue, life-sequencing issue, sex-role issue, and practical issues.

The **marital issue** is the first to be discussed. Marriage involves the coming together of two people to form one unique relationship. It also involves a set of cultural traditions. Married couples are guided by these traditions that have been handed down from generation to generation. At least for middle-class families, the ideal has been a one-worker family in which the male is the breadwinner and the female is the homemaker.

Dual-worker families challenge these traditions and are creating new ones. What is the blueprint for a dual-worker family? What are the norms or modes of behavior that are acceptable in this form of marriage? Because this is a relatively new pattern of marital life, there are no models to follow. It is the married couples who engage in this marital style who are creating the traditions for future generations.

The **childrearing issue** is of central importance in discussions of dual-worker families. There is an ongoing debate over how the phenomenon of working mothers affects children. Of course, at least in the past, questions about the father's parenting responsibilities have been omitted from these discussions. One of the interesting aspects of the increase in dual-worker families is that more research is now being done on fathering.

If both parents work, childrearing becomes an important issue. Research does show a greater use of day-care centers, and to some degree increasing numbers of fathers are taking on child-care responsibilities. The presence of children affects marital relationships and issues related to marital equality. If there are no children present, the two-worker family tends to be relatively egalitarian with husband and wife sharing power and decision making. However, if children are present, the wife tends to take on greater responsibility for child care, and this affects the degree of egalitarianism in the marriage. There appears to be less egalitarianism if children are present.

With respect to the impact of this marital style on children, the evidence is somewhat mixed. There is no clear consensus as to whether or not the children of dual-worker families are better or worse off. If either or both parents are experiencing stress on the job, then the child, too, may suffer. On the other hand, if both parents work, there may be less likelihood that the family will be living in poverty and the child certainly will benefit from that. Some research indicates that there is a positive effect on girls when their mothers work. With their working mom as a role model, these daughters tend to have higher aspirations for themselves.

The **homemaker issue** is the third issue. Who takes care of the house? Traditionally, of course, this was seen as the woman's role. Research indicates that men are beginning to take some of the responsibility for tending to household chores, but almost all of the research indicates that women still do most of the homemaking work. For example, men may take out the garbage, but, by and large, women clean the house and prepare dinner and then clean up the house again after sixteen relatives have come for a visit.

Today, more families try to mitigate this by making use of external resources such as cleaning services or take-out restaurants. The feasibility of these solutions, however, is determined by the social class of the two-worker family. If both the husband and wife make minimal salaries, they cannot afford to use such resources. Middle-class couples will be more likely to be able to afford these services.

The **workplace issue,** in a practical sense, may be the most difficult issue for the couple because the power lies outside the couple. Specifically, how does each member of the couple negotiate his or her workplace so that both can fully participate in a dual-worker marriage? Can either party go to the boss and say, "Well, I have to leave the office for three hours because I have to see my child's teacher and it's my turn to take care of this parental responsibility." Some bosses, of course, may be very understanding, but in general the workplace is not supportive of this marital lifestyle. Again, it may fall to the wife/mother to take care of this type of issue, and thus it may be her work path that is negatively affected by such situations. Couples sometimes have to be very innovative in their approach to work in order to find some balance between work and family responsibilities.

Related to the workplace issue is the **life-sequencing issue.** Both husband and wife are in the labor force, but this does not mean that they have the same job or the same experiences. They each will have their own career path and sometimes their paths may not be synchronized. For example, it is customary for older men to marry younger women. Wives may be two or three or more years younger than their spouses. This is important because some men may wish to retire at fifty-five. Their wives may be only fifty-two at the time and have no wish to retire. This is a life-sequencing issue. The husband and wife both work but they are at different stages in their career. The husband may want his wife to retire so she can join him in his retirement. But she may not wish to retire because she has seven or more years of productive work.

Another variation of this theme may involve geographic mobility. Again, assuming the husband is older by three years, let us say he is thirty and well established in his job or career and has already achieved a relatively high position that requires him to stay where he is. The wife, at twenty-seven years, may still be growing in her career. What if she gets a promotion, but at another office that is one thousand miles away? The issue is obvious: do they move or not? Do they establish, as some couples do, what is called a bicoastal marriage in which one party lives on one coast, and the other on the other coast?

A sixth issue is the **sex-role issue.** This has often been discussed with respect to the husband's attitude toward the wife working. How difficult is it for some men to adjust to this reality? The belief some have is that a man's sense of masculinity is challenged by his wife's working. He does not feel like a "real" man. This may have been true in the 1960s and 1970s. It seems likely that it is less true today. Men have had almost an entire generation to adjust to this new pattern.

It is more interesting to examine how women are reacting to the emergence of their new role vis-à-vis the idea of women's work. Many women may be experiencing an internal conflict with regard to their self-defined sex role because they were raised in households where traditional sex roles were the norm. They were exposed to gender-based childrearing when their mothers taught them by both word and deed that "girls should clean the house, wash the dishes, and cook the meals" and they internalized this idea of womanhood.

Today many of these women are trying to balance both work and family. Their idealized version of womanhood is what they were raised to believe, but their real life as women is much different. Their sex-role socialization process does not reflect what their adult lives are really like. Thus, they may come to have an internal conflict between the idea of what they were supposed to become and what they really became. I believe that this conflict may cut across class lines. Whether the woman is a cashier, secretary, lawyer, or physician may not matter. For some women, no matter how far they advance in their professional lives, they may feel some sense of guilt because of the ideas they were exposed to during childhood.

This brings us to the last issue: **practical issues.** There are a variety of practical issues couples in dual-worker families may have to face, but I will discuss only two of these. First is the issue of **time.** In research on such couples, one of the major complaints they voice is concern over time. For them, there never seems to be enough time in the day to do all the things they feel they have to do. Working, shopping, cleaning, cooking, and, if there are children, all the obligations linked to parenting all seem to be too much. What is suggested in the literature is that such couples need to create a **hierarchy of values.** Everything may seem important, but couples need to determine, in discussions with each other, what is more important. They need to prioritize all the things they need or want to do.

A second practical issue is the impact this marital style has on the couple's **social and family network.** Because time is so precious, there may be less time to interact with family and friends. This extended network may not understand especially if the individuals' lifestyle is different from the one we are discussing. They may lack empathy, or simply not understand how the couple could not have time to call or write or see them, and the dual-worker couple may feel that they have little support outside of their nuclear family. It is important for such couples to try to help others see why such contact may be problematic in light of the lifestyle they are leading.

These are some of the issues facing couples in dual-worker families. Are there any benefits? There are **three benefits** we can cite. First, and perhaps the most obvious, the couple has two incomes. We know that economic problems are associated with a variety of other problems including marital stress, difficulties for the children, and a sense of personal failure. With two incomes, even for working-class families, some of these issues are mitigated by the presence of the second income.

The second benefit is related to a **sense of self.** Work has a psychological benefit in addition to the economic benefit. In the United States, people derive a sense of self from their work. One can feel that one is an accomplished adult because of the work. This holds true regardless of the nature of the work. This holds important benefits for the marriage because if one has a positive sense of self then the marital relationship will benefit as well. Because they both work, the couple may have a variety of things to discuss over dinner. They may be able to empathize with each other because, regardless of the specific nature of the work, there are general characteristics they can share.

Third, evidence suggests that when both parties work there may be a greater chance for the development of an **egalitarian marriage** in which both parties share in the decision making. It reduces the potential for abuse, either physical or emotional. Such a marriage may help both parties feel more fulfilled and, in simpler terms, happier.

In the analysis section, you will have the opportunity to examine some of the general characteristics of dual-worker families including such key variables as education and income.

Analysis

TABLE 11.1 *Married Couple Family Groups (in thousands) by Labor Force Status: March 2000*

Labor Force Status	Number	Percent
All married couples	56,497	100.0
Both employed	30,212	
Only husband employed	11,884	
Only wife employed	3,234	
Neither in labor force	9,288	

Source: U.S. Census Bureau, *Married Couple Family Groups, by Labor Force Status of Both Spouses, and Race and Hispanic Origin of the Reference Person: March 2000,* www.census.gov/population/socdemo/hh-fam/p20-537/2000/tabFG1.txt

1. How many two-worker families are there in the United States? Table 11.1 presents the total number of married couples by work category. Calculate the percentage distribution of married couples in each of the work categories and put your answers in the table. Note that the percentage will not equal 100.0 because unemployment categories are not included.

2. Based on your calculations, what general statement can you make about two-worker families?

3. The category "only husband employed" is about four times greater than "only wife employed." Why is this the case?

TABLE 11.2   *Regional Distribution of Two-Worker Families (in thousands): March 2000*

Region	All Married Couples	Both Employed	Percentage of Both Employed
Northeast	10,349	5,580	
Midwest	13,330	7,609	
South	20,529	10,788	
West	12,289	6,236	

Source: U.S. Census Bureau, *Married Couple Family Groups, by Labor Force Status of Both Spouses, and Race and Hispanic Origin of the Reference Person: March 2000,* www.census.gov/population/socdemo/hh-fam/p20-537/2000/tabFG1.txt

4. In Table 11.2 data is presented on regional differences in two-worker families. Calculate the percentage of two-worker families in each region and put your answers in the table.

5. What statement can you make that holds true for all four regions?

6. Which region has the highest percentage of "both employed"?

7. Why do you believe this is the case?

TABLE 11.3   *Percentage of Both Employed by Area of Residence*

Area of Residence	All Married Couples	No. of Both Employed	Percentage
Central cities	13,532	6,924	51.2
Suburban	31,048	17,052	54.9
Rural	11,917	6,237	52.3

Source: Adapted from U.S. Census Bureau, *Married Couple Family Groups, by Labor Force Status of Both Spouses, and Race and Hispanic Origin of the Reference Person: March 2000,* www.census.gov/population/socdemo/hh-fam/p20-537/2000/tabFG1.txt

8. Table 11.3 presents data on two-worker families and the area they live in. Typically, researchers look for a difference of ±3 percent to indicate significant differences in the data. Are there significant differences in the percentage of two-worker families by area of residence?

9. What might account for the lack of differences?

10. Given the data in Tables 11.2 and 11.3, what general conclusions can you draw about two-worker families in the United States?

TABLE 11.4 *Number and Percentage of Two-Worker Families by Age of Own Children: March 2000*

Age of Children	All Married Couples	Both Employed	Percentage of Both Employed
Under 1 year	2,350	1,176	
Under 3 years	7,002	3,794	
Under 5 years	10,248	5,795	
Under 6 years	11,711	6,752	
Under 12 years	19,519	12,044	
Under 18 years	25,771	16,584	

Source: U.S. Census Bureau, *Married Couple Family Groups, by Labor Force Status of Both Spouses, and Race and Hispanic Origin of the Reference Person: March 2000,* www.census.gov/population/socdemo/hh-fam/p20-537/2000/tabFG1.txt

11. The presence of children may affect two-worker family patterns. Table 11.4 presents data on the number of two-worker families by the age of their children. Calculate the percentage distribution of two-worker families for each age of children category and put your answers in the table.

12. What pattern emerges from your calculations?

13. What factors do you believe influence the emergence of this pattern?

TABLE 11.5 *Educational Differences of Husbands and Wives: March 2000*

Educational Difference	Number	Percent
Husband more education than wife	13,843	24.5
Husband and wife same education	30,590	54.1
Wife more education than husband	12,064	21.4

Source: U.S. Census Bureau, *Married Couple Family Groups, by Presence of Own Children under 18, and Age, Earnings, Education, and Race and Hispanic Origin of Both Spouses: March 2000,* www.census.gov/population/socdemo/hh-fam/p20-537/2000/tabFG3.txt

14. One major reason for the increase in two-worker families is economics. Let us examine the income factor. Before doing that, though, let us take a brief look at education because education influences income. Table 11.5 presents data on educational differences between husbands and wives. What general observations can be made from the data?

TABLE 11.6   *Earnings Difference for All Married Couples with and without Own Children under 18 Years of Age (in percentages): March 2000*

Earnings Difference	All Married Couples	Without Own Children under 18	With Own Children under 18
Husband earns $50,000+ more	15.5	11.5	20.2
Husband earns $30,000–$49,999 more	14.1	10.8	17.9
Husband earns $10,000–$29,999 more	23.4	18.5	29.1
Husband earns $5,000–$9,999 more	5.9	5.3	6.7
Husband earns within $4,999 of wife	26.3	37.4	13.0
Wife earns $5,000–$9,999 more	3.8	3.7	3.8
Wife earns $10,000–$29,999 more	7.3	8.2	6.2
Wife earns $30,000–$49,999 more	2.5	2.9	2.0
Wife earns $50,000+ more	1.3	1.5	1.1

Source: U.S. Census Bureau, *Married Couple Family Groups, by Presence of Own Children under 18, and Age, Earnings, Education, and Race and Hispanic Origin of Both Spouses: March 2000,* www.census.gov/population/socdemo/hh-fam/p20-537/2000/tabFG3.txt

15. Now let us turn to income. Table 11.6 presents data on income for all married couples and includes data for those couples with and without children under the age of eighteen years. Examine the data carefully. As a point of information, the **mode** is the number that appears most often in a set of numbers. A **modal category** is the category that has the highest percentage in a distribution of numbers. Now find the modal category for "All Married Couples."

16. What is the modal category for married couples without their own children under eighteen years of age?

17. What is the modal category for married couples with their own children under eighteen years of age?

18. How do you explain the differences in the modal categories?

19. In general, what comparisons can you make for the differences in husband and wife earnings?

20. How does the presence of children affect the earnings difference?

21. What marital issues might arise from these differences?

22. What are some advantages of being in a two-worker marriage?

23. What are some of the disadvantages of being in a two-worker marriage?

Selected Bibliography and Suggested Readings _____

Aldous, Joan. (Ed.). (1982). *Two paychecks: Life in dual-earner families*. Beverly Hills: Sage.

Crosby, Faye. (1991). *Juggling: The unexpected advantages of balancing career and home for women and their families*. New York: Free Press.

Deutsch, Francine. (1999). *Halving it all: How equally shared parenting works*. Cambridge: Harvard University Press.

Hertz, Rosanna. (1986). *More equal than others: Women and men in dual-career marriages*. Berkeley: University of California Press.

Mahony, Rhona. (1995). *Kidding ourselves: Breadwinning, babies, and bargaining power*. New York: Basic Books.

Pepitone-Rockwell, Fran. (Ed.). (1980). *Dual-career couples*. Beverly Hills: Sage.

Potuchek, J. (1997). *Who supports the family? Gender and breadwinning in dual-earner marriages*. Stanford, CA: Stanford University Press.

Rapoport, Rhona, & Rapoport, Robert. (Eds.). (1978). *Working couples*. New York: Harper & Row.

Smith, Audrey, & Reid, William. (1986). *Role-sharing marriage*. New York: Columbia University Press.

Swiss, Deborah, & Walker, Judith. (1993). *Women and the work/family dilemma: How today's professional women are finding solutions*. New York: Wiley.

Wertheimer, Barbara. (1977). *We were there: The story of working women in America*. New York: Pantheon.

12

Single Parenting:
I Can't Be in Three Place
at the Same Time

In the past forty years the fastest growing type of family has been the single-parent family. This is due to two major related trends. The first is the increase in the number of divorces in the United States (see Chapter 6). The second is the increase in the number of never-married mothers and fathers. Both factors have contributed to the substantial increase in single parenting. In 1960 there were close to six million children in single-parent homes. Today, the figure is almost twenty million children. Seventy percent of these children are living with either a never-married parent or a divorced parent.

There is little question that greater numbers of adults and children find themselves in this kind of family today. How does this lifestyle affect both the adults and children? Let us examine the impact on the adults first. There are three general effects of single parenting on the adult–parent: multitasking, flying solo, and issues of self.

Multitasking, a term derived from computer technology, refers to the multiple demands placed on single parents. Single parents may have to play a variety of roles simultaneously—parent, child, student, employee, friend, and so on. Just as a computer may be called on to work at a variety of tasks at the same time, the same may hold true for the single parent. This may lead to **role conflict**. Role conflict exists when there are competing demands made on us. For example, a single parent may be at work or in school and receive a message from the child's school that an emergency has arisen and his or her presence is required at the school. In this case, the parent is in conflict because there are demands from both the parental role and the worker role. Role conflict and multitasking issues appear to be common in the life of the single parent.

The second issue in single parenting is **solo parenting.** While the point may be debatable, many social observers argue that it is more difficult to parent today. Even for two-parent families, parenting may be more arduous than it was in the past. There is an expectation that all parents must be "perfect." They are supposed to supply the financial, emotional, and intellectual supports that their children will need to grow up to be emotionally healthy and financially successful adults.

In addition, parents face a variety of competitors for their children's attention, and some of these competitors may not seem all that positive. There is television, rock music, and, most importantly, their children's peers. Some argue that children today face peer pressure at earlier and earlier ages. "Keeping up with the Joneses" may be an old-fashioned expression, but it may be more meaningful today than in the past. Children are expected to keep up with respect to their grades in school, their social and athletic skills, or, perhaps more generally, to keep up with "being cool," however that is defined by the peer group. They are exposed to a variety of behavior patterns, some of which may not be viewed as positive by the parent. For example, exposure to drug use and changing sexual **mores** or **norms** is probably occurring at younger ages.

For a single parent, confronting these issues may be more difficult because there may be no one with whom to share and discuss these potential problems. Single parents are often the only adults present in the child's life, and it is the single parent who must make important and meaningful decisions that will influence the child's future behavior. If there is no one to share the parenting issues, it means the single parent must bear a greater burden than that of two-parent families, which can lead to greater levels of self-doubt and uncertainty. Some evidence suggests that it may also lead to a more authoritarian approach to parenting. Because of the inability or lack of opportunity to "escape" from parenting responsibilities, some single parents may become more authoritarian. They do not have the time or patience to reason with their child(ren) as issues arise.

At the same time it may place a greater burden on the children to make their own decisions, and this may not be all that bad. Children of single parents may mature at an earlier age, develop good decision-making skills, and come to be more independent and self-reliant.

The third area of concern for the adults in single-parent families is the **issue of self.** Parents are people, too. This may sound overly simplistic, but it is a reality that is often overlooked. While there has been much discussion about the effects of single parenting on children, there has been relatively little discussion of the effects on the parent. The adult living this experience may also be under stress, and his or her own needs may be largely ignored. The adult may wish to continue his or her education, work at a job, and have a social life. Single parents may lack a very important element in his or her life, and that is time for themselves.

This lac   f time for themselves, with the potential for negative experiences and tl   levelopment of a negative sense of self, can have an impact
on the childi   . Research indicates that positive parenting is associated
with parents   o have a positive self-image. If the adult does not have the
opportunity t   row and develop positive experiences for himself or herself, then the   lity of parenting will diminish. For example, research indicates that if   e single parent has the opportunity to further his or her
education, anc   that person can then develop a good career path, there
will be a variet   f benefits for the children. The children will do better in
school and be l   likely to experience the negative consequences often associated with si   le-parent households.

There has   en much research and debate on the impact of single-
parent homes or   hildren. This is especially true with regard to the study of
divorce on chilc   n, although there is no scholarly consensus as to the
long-term effects   Many scholars believe that short-term effects tend to be
negative, but eve   this observation is debated. The short-term effects may
be mediated by a   umber of factors including the age and sex of the child
(see Chapter 6). T   s discussion will explore two elements in the attempt to
understand the in   act of single parenting on children: **the economic** and
the emotional.

A number o   esearchers argue that many of the negative consequences for childr   in single-parent homes may be traced to **economic
problems.** Womer   read many single-parent households, and many of
these households a   near or under the poverty line. While the numbers
fluctuate from yea   to year, about 60 percent of female-headed single-
parent households l   e near or below the poverty line. There are, however,
some differences wi   respect to the marital status of the mother. Almost
70 percent of all chil   en raised by never-married mothers, compared to 45
percent of children r   sed by divorced mothers, live near or below the poverty line. To further   mplicate the analysis, many of these women were
poor before they had   hildren.

An issue related   economic well-being for divorced persons is **child
support.** Child suppo   may be awarded to the custodial parent in a divorce
proceeding. This is m   ey allotted for the support of the child by the noncustodial parent. In 1   5, 58 percent of all custodial parents were awarded
child support. Most of these awards are legal agreements made through the
courts or other government agencies. The actual amount of money received averaged about $300.00 per month in 1995, and, interestingly, was
about the same for either a mother or father custodial parent. Receiving
child support does seem to affect financial status. Of those custodial parents who did receive at least some child support, about 22 percent were
below the poverty line. For those parents who were supposed to but did not
receive child support payments, 32 percent lived below the poverty line.
For those custodial parents who were not awarded child support, their
number below the poverty line was almost 36 percent.

One often hears that children from single-parent households are more likely to do poorly in school, have excess truancy, use alcohol and/or drugs, and become involved in delinquent or criminal behavior. All these behaviors are associated with poverty as well. Therefore, the scholarly question is: are these behaviors the result of poverty or of single parenting? One might "cop-out" and say that it is a combination of both factors that contributes to these behaviors. At this point in time, however, research has reached no clear answers. It should also be pointed out that there are many children from single-parent households who grow up with relatively little difficulty. At the same time, there are children who grow up in two-parent households who experience a variety of problems.

The second area of concern is the **emotional impact** of single parenting on children. Do children need two parents to develop in an emotionally healthy manner? This is a thorny question because it is sometimes difficult to assess what is meant by "emotionally healthy."

There is a general consensus that all children need a warm, loving, and nurturing environment within which to grow and mature. What the structure of this environment should be is what is subject to debate. Is it necessary to have an adult of each sex? Are biological parents the best parents? Can a child develop in an emotionally healthy manner if grandparents (see Chapter 13) raise him or her?

It would seem to be the case that the quality of childrearing is more important than the structure. What may be very important for children of single parents is the **total support network.** Is there an extended kin network to offer support, guidance, and nurturance to the child? Such support would also benefit the single parent. Many of the issues related to the adult discussed previously may be mediated by the presence of other adults to take the pressure off the single parent.

The emotional response of children to the single-parent lifestyle is a product of a variety of variables including such factors as sex of the child and the sex of the custodial parent, social class, education of the parent, and a host of other factors. At this point, there appears to be no definitive statement. It may be the case that single parenting is as varied as two-parent parenting is. One should be cautious in trying to draw general conclusions for an entire class of family systems.

Single parenting contributes to another trend in the United States: the increase in the number of stepparents. **Stepparenting** is an interesting sociological phenomenon. There is certainly nothing new about stepparenting; it has existed throughout history. In the past stepparenting was largely a result of the death of a biological parent and the remarriage of the surviving parent. Today, it is largely a result of remarriage after divorce or the marriage of a never-married parent.

Researchers estimate that approximately 50 percent of all children will spend some of their childhood with a nonbiological parent. To get a sense of how stepparents have been perceived, one need go no further than som of our fairy tales. In many such tales there is the classic character of the "evil" stepparent. From a sociological perspective, what is interesting about stepparenting is the fact that there are no clear-cut norms that can serve as models for behavior. Most people have some sense of what it means to be a parent. There are guidelines and expectations of behavior for those who come to play this role. Stepparenting is an entirely different story. For example, we expect biological parents to play the role of disciplinarian. Stepparents, however, may face a more difficult time when they try to discipline a stepchild who responds: "Don't tell me what to do, you're not my father (mother)!"

Given the historically high rates of single parenting, it is relatively easy to predict that more and more adults will find themselves in the role of stepparent. It may be the case that those adults who are now playing this role will create the norms for others who will follow. Certainly it will be the interplay of stepchild and stepparent that will come to define what is expected and appropriate for both parties in this emerging family relationship.

The analysis section of this chapter will give you the opportunity to examine some of the changing patterns of single parenting. Changes in the number of children living with single parents will be explored, along with shifting patterns of the sex of the single parent. In addition, the impact of single parenting on economic well-being will also be analyzed.

Analysis

TABLE 12.1 Children under 18 Years Old Living with One Parent by Custodial Parent (in thousands): 1960 to 2000

Year	Total N	Mother Only		Father Only	
		Number	Percent	Number	Percent
1960	63,727	5,105		724	
1970	70,213	7,678		760	
1980	63,427	11,406		1,060	
1990	64,137	13,874		1,993	
2000	72,012	16,162		3,058	

Source: U.S. Census Bureau, *Living Arrangements of Children under 18 Years Old: 1960 to Present.* Release date: June 29, 2001, www.census.gov/population/socdemo/hh-fam/tabCH-1.txt

1. How many children are living with single parents? Table 12.1 presents the numbers of children living with only one parent. Calculate the percentage of children living with their mother or father for the years indicated and put your answers in the table.

2. What general patterns do you find in the data?

3. Which decade witnessed the greatest change?

4. Why do you believe this decade experienced the greatest increase?

5. Next, examine the overall changes between 1960 and 2000. You can do this by looking at percentage change over time utilizing the following formula:

$$\frac{2000 - 1960}{1960} \times 100 = \text{Percent change 1960 to 2000}$$

a. Now calculate the increase in the percentage of all children (total number) _____

b. Children living with mother only _____

c. Children living with father only _____

6. Discuss the differences in the rates of change.

TABLE 12.2   *Children under 18 Years Old Living with Mother Only by Marital Status of Mother (in thousands): 1960 to 2000*

	1960	*1970*	*1980*	*1990*	*2000*
Total no. of children living with mother only	5,105	7,678	11,131	13,874	16,162
Marital status of mother					
No. divorced	1,210	2,338	4,766	5,118	5,655
Percent divorced					
No. married, spouse absent	2,363	3,351	3,610	3,416	3,224
Percent married, spouse absent					
No. widowed	1,311	1,421	1,286	975	692
Percent widowed					
No. never married	221	565	1,745	4,365	6,591
Percent never married					

Source: U.S. Census Bureau, *Children under 18 Years Living with Mother Only by Marital Status of Mother.* Release date: June 29, 2001, www.census.gov/population/socdemo/hh-fam/tabCH-5.txt

7. Single parenthood may be the result of several different factors. Table 12.2 presents data for children living only with their mother and the marital status of the mother. Calculate the percentage distribution by marital status of the mother and put your answers in the table.

8. Which two marital status categories experienced the greatest growth?

9. What factors may have contributed to this pattern?

TABLE 12.3 *Children under 18 Years Old Living with Father Only by Marital Status of Father (in thousands): 1960 to 2000*

	1960	*1970*	*1980*	*1990*	*2000*
Total no. of children living with father only	724	748	1,031	1,993	3,058
Marital status of father					
No. divorced	129	177	515	1,004	1,330
Percent divorced					
No. married, spouse absent	348	287	288	351	570
Percent married, spouse absent					
No. widowed	229	254	183	150	153
Percent widowed					
No. never married	22	32	75	488	1,006
Percent never married					

Source: U.S. Census Bureau, *Children under 18 Years Living with Mother Only by Marital Status of Mother.* Release date: June 29, 2001, www.census.gov/population/socdemo/hh-fam/tabCH-6.txt

10. In Table 12.3 do the same calculations for children living only with their fathers.

11. Which two marital status categories show the greatest increase?

12. What factors might explain this pattern?

13. Describe the similarities and differences between the data in Tables 12.2 and 12.3.

TABLE 12.4   *Distribution of Family Income by Type of Family (in thousands): March 2000*

Income	All Families		Mother Only		Father Only	
	Number	Percent	Number	Percent	Number	Percent
Total no.	75,581		9,681		2,044	
Under $14,999	9,345		4,289		451	
$15,000–24,999	9,400		2,180		400	
$25,000–39,999	13,308		1,708		489	
$40,000–74,999	23,330		1,192		501	
$75,000 and over	20,198		312		203	

Source: U.S. Census Bureau, *America's Families and Living Arrangements: 2000,* June 2001, pp. 20–537; *One-Parent Family Groups with own Children under 18…* www.census.gov/population/socdemo/hh-fam/p20–537/2000/tabFG5.txt

14. One major issue related to single parenting is economic disadvantage. Let us see how single-parent families compare to all families with respect to family income. Table 12.4 presents data on family income for all families, mother-only families and father-only families. Calculate the percentage of families that fall into each income category and put your answers in the table.

15. How do mother-only families compare to father-only families with respect to income patterns?

16. How do single-parent families compare to all families?

17. What are some of the implications of the income patterns you discovered in the data?

Selected Bibliography and Suggested Readings _____

Bianchi, S., & Casper, L. (2000, December). American families. *Population Bulletin*. Washington, DC: Population Reference Bureau.

Ludtke, M. (1997). *On our own: Unmarried motherhood in America*. New York: Random House.

Maynard, R. (Ed.). (1997). *Kids having kids: Economic costs and social consequences of teen pregnancy*. Washington, DC: Urban Institute Press.

McLanahan, S., & Sandefur, G. (1994). *Growing up with a single parent: What hurts, what helps*. Cambridge, MA: Harvard University Press.

Reigot, B., & Spina, R. (1996). *Beyond the traditional family: Voices of diversity*. New York: Springer.

Scoon-Rogers, Lydia. (1999, March). Child support for custodial mothers and fathers: 1995. *Current Population Reports*, 60–195.

Sugarman, Stephen. (2001). Single-parent families. In Susan Ferguson (Ed.), *Shifting the center: Understanding contemporary families* (2nd ed., pp. 238–250). Mountain View, CA: Mayfield.

U.S. Census Bureau. Children with single parents—How they fare. *Census Brief*, CENBR/97-1, September 1997.

13

The Aged Population: The Emergence of Grandparenting

The twentieth century witnessed a number of dramatic changes. Advances in technology and medical care, along with new weapons of mass destruction, are all products of this past century. Social norms changed with shifts in perceptions of women, lowering fertility rates, and changes in sexual behavior. One of the more important changes that has received less notoriety than the others is the change in life expectancy.

In the year 1900 about one out of twenty-five Americans were sixty-five years of age or over. As of 2000, the proportion of elderly has risen to one out of eight, or 12.4 percent of the entire population. There are almost 35 million persons in this age category. In fact, there are currently almost 17 million persons seventy-five years and older, while there are 19 million persons under the age of five. Our oldest age cohort is almost as large as our youngest age cohort.

Another way to examine the changes in life expectancy is to look at the median age of the total population. Remember that the median is the midpoint in a set of numbers. In 1900, the median age of the population was 22.9 years. This means that 50 percent of the population was over 22.9 years and 50 percent of the population was under 22.9 years. In 2000, the median age of the population was 35.3 years. In fact, since 1820 (with a median age of 16.7), there has been a steady increase in the median age with the exception of 1960 to 1980, when the baby boom and its accompanying high fertility rates lowered the median age.

These data indicate that the United States is an aging society. This is not unique to the United States. Many of the more developed societies, such as those in Europe, are experiencing this same aging pattern. Life expectancy is now close to eighty years for females and almost seventy-five years for men in the United States, and some other developed countries have even higher life expectancies.

Perhaps even more significant is the fact that, if one reaches the age of sixty-five years, one has, on average, another eighteen years of life. These demographic data are the underpinnings of an interesting, but sometimes overlooked phenomenon in our society, the emergence of grandparenting. One of the myths of family life is the belief that, in the past, three-generations households were common. This is a myth because in the past there were not many grandparents. With relatively low life expectancy, very few children ever saw their grandparents. On a personal note, for example, I never saw either of my grandfathers. They both died even before my parents married, and that was not an unusual occurrence for their generation.

Today it is much more common for children to have grandparents. Evidence indicates that grandparents are vital members of the extended kin network of children. A recent survey by the American Association of Retired Persons (AARP) revealed that four out of five grandparents had at least spoken to their grandchild in the previous month, and about 70 percent had shared a meal with their grandchild.

This chapter will present a brief overview of the grandparenting experience. There is no one type of grandparent and substantial variation in grandparenting relationships. Different researchers have developed different grandparent typologies. What follows is a summary of several different typologies. The **grandparent typology** includes the following: family historian, mentor, entertainer, formal grandparent, aloof grandparent, and counselor.

The **family historian** is the grandparent who enjoys telling stories about the family's past. She or he may be the repository of the family's history and relishes passing on this information to the younger generation. Younger grandchildren may not appreciate this information, but as they get older they feel sometimes sorry they were not as attentive as they should have been.

The **mentor** is the family elder others look up to and want to emulate. She or he is a teacher who serves as a role model for others. Similar to the mentor is the **counselor** and, in many cases, the grandparent combines both roles. The counselor is a good listener. She or he mediates conflicts between parents and child. This person has a good set of ears and gives the child an alternative to the parent. Although this may be a very difficult role to play, the grandparent may serve as a mediator between parent and child.

The **entertainer** is the fun-loving grandparent. This person is typically a source of great joy for the grandchild. This is the grandparent who tells jokes or wonderful stories. This grandparent is the child's "pal." Somewhat the opposite of the entertainer is the **formal grandparent.** As the term implies, this grandparent is very formal and "proper" in his or her interaction with the child. They don't seem to let loose. This type of grandparent was, in all likelihood, also a formal parent.

The **aloof grandparent** is the grandparent who has only infrequent contact with the child. This may be due to individual personality characteristics, issues related to their own child or their in-laws, or this grandparent may be the parent of a divorced child who is the noncustodial parent.

How do these various types of grandparenting styles emerge? A key factor, of course, is the relationship the grandparent had with his or her own children. This three-generation relationship constitutes a **triad**, with each generation influencing the relationship with all other generations. If a grandparent has a difficult relationship with his or her own child, this may sour the relationship with the grandchild. Grandchildren, on the other hand, develop strategies as to how to interact with their grandparents by observing how their own parents interact with them.

In addition to these internal dynamics, the larger culture will also influence the interaction patterns. Variables such as social class, race, religion, and ethnic background may all influence the triadic relationship. Cultural perceptions of the elderly will also play a role. It seems to be the case that in the United States there has been a sea change in perceptions of the elderly. In the past, elderly people were seen as *old*. This may seem odd, so allow me to explain. Years ago the elderly were older in their behavior. Perhaps because of closer ties to traditional notions of the elderly, they were to be revered. You would not see the entertainer type of grandparent as often as the formal or aloof type.

Today many grandparents are what one researcher terms the "young-old." People sixty-five years and over are in many ways more youthful than their counterparts in the past. They are certainly healthier and are often better educated as well. The culture's entire perception of old age is changing. This may be due to the large numbers of baby boomers who are beginning to enter this stage of life. To put it in a historical context, this emerging grandparent generation was there when rock 'n' roll began in the 1950s. They were fans of Elvis Presley, and later on the Beatles and the Rolling Stones. They listened to Bob Dylan, and participated in the Civil Rights Movement, the Women's Movement, and debates about society's involvement in the Vietnam War.

They are also a generation that is the wealthiest the society has ever produced. In large measure because of their high level of educational attainment and the expanding economy, this generation is better prepared to retire than any generation before. It understands the importance of 401Ks and IRAs and other retirement products. Perhaps because they understood that, unlike previous generations, there was a much greater likelihood that they would have a longer retirement, they took greater care to plan for it. The reader, however, should not misinterpret this information. There are still elderly members of the U.S. society who are not well off economically.

A number of elderly are poor, although the proportion of elderly who are poor is not as great as was the case in the past. What all this means is that the emerging generation of grandparents has both the physical and economic resources to be more active in the lives of their grandchildren.

Because the potential to grandparent is greater today than in the past, the question then arises as to how to integrate oneself into the life of the grandchild. One important issue that may be contentious is parenting styles. Grandparents and parents may disagree about the strategies being utilized by the parents. The reverse may also hold true. For example, the grandparents may wish to give things—money, toys, and so forth—to the grandchildren, but the parents may interpret this as spoiling the child. What constitutes "giving" and "spoiling" is not clearly delineated. It seems to be a matter of one's point of view. However, real disputes can arise over this very issue.

What is interesting is the underlying dynamics. The grandparent is still the parent of the parent. Your own children may be different parents than you were; their children are certainly different than were your own children. There are not only different personalities involved, but also different generations. Each generation is a product of a different cultural milieu with different values, beliefs, and, certainly, with different experiences. This three-generation triad then has the potential for much friction. What is surprising is that there is little evidence that much friction occurs. Most grandparents, when surveyed, appear to be quite happy in their grandparenting role.

The most intensive form of grandparenting is when the grandparents take on the parenting role full-time: the **grandparent as parent (GAP)**. This kind of relationship is often seen as an oddity or at the very least somewhat unusual. It is often the result of a tragic set of circumstances: the biological parent has died, a young unwed mother is incapable of raising the child, the parent is incapacitated by physical or emotional illness, there is substance abuse, or one or both parents are incarcerated. In some cases, GAP may not be the result of a tragedy of such dimensions, but may be due to situations in which both parents work, and work long hours. It may be due to divorce, and the custodial parent must work to support the family. In any case, GAP appears to be somewhat of a social anomaly. There is relatively little social support for such grandparents and their legal rights are unclear.

There have been a number of recent legal cases involving the legal rights of grandparents, but the courts have not sent any clear message as to these legal rights. In some cases the grandparent(s) may be granted **physical custody** of a child, and the child lives with the grandparents. There is also the issue of **legal custody**—who has the right to make legal decisions for the child. Grandparents may also seek or be assigned **guardianship**, which typically involves temporary physical and legal custody. In some cases grandparents may **adopt** their own grandchildren, which results in permanent physical and legal custody. All of these resolutions involve a difficult and perhaps costly legal process. In most states the court cases indicate that courts favor parents over grandparents, even in cases involving visitation rights. If custody is at issue, this will be even more difficult for the grandparent to attain. Because this is largely an emerging form of family, the legal process will evolve over time.

There are several positive and negative attributes of GAP. Positive attributes include helping the child to grow and mature and the emotional benefits derived from this experience. Raising a child may also help the grandparents stay, or at least feel, young. Being around young people may stimulate their feeling of well-being. In some cases, raising the grandchild also benefits one's own child if he or she needs to work, or if he or she is going through some difficult period.

Negative attributes may include the economic hardships involved in trying to raise a child. Bringing the child in may alter the grandparents' own retirement plans. As the grandparent ages, health issues may arise, and his or her capability of raising the child may be questioned. For many grandparents put in this position, the situation can be a mixed blessing.

In the next section of this chapter you will be given the opportunity to examine changes in the elderly population, and to analyze some of the issues related to GAP.

Analysis

TABLE 13.1 *Total Number of People and People 65 or Older (in millions): 1950 to 2000*

Year	Total Population	65 or Older	Percent Elderly
1950	151.3	12.3	
1960	179.3	16.6	
1970	203.3	20.1	
1980	226.3	25.5	
1990	248.7	31.2	
2000	281.4	35.0	

Source: U.S. Census Bureau, *Statistical Abstract of the United States: 2000,* Table 1; *Profile of General Demographic Characteristics: 2000,* Census 2000; U.S. National Vital Statistics System, *Federal Interagency Forum on Aging Related Statistics,* www.agingstats...artbook2000/tables-population.html

1. First, examine what proportion of the population is made up of the elderly. Table 13.1 presents data on the total population of the United States from 1950 to 2000. Calculate what percentage of the population is sixty-five years of age and over for the years shown in the table and put your answers in the space provided.

2. Describe the pattern you found in the table.

3. Another way to analyze the data is to compare the rate of increase of the total population to the rate of increase of the aged population. Between 1950 and 2000 what has been the rate of increase for the total population? Remember that to calculate this rate of increase you would use the following formula:

$$\frac{2000 - 1950}{1950} \times 100 = \text{rate of increase (same as percentage increase)}$$

4. What has been the rate of increase for the aged population?

5. How would you compare these two rates?

TABLE 13.2 *Life Expectancy at Birth and at Age 65: 1900 to 2000*

	1900	*1950*	*2000*
Life expectancy at birth			
Total	49.2	68.1	76.9
Men	47.9	65.5	74.1
Women	50.7	71.0	79.5
Life expectancy at age 65			
Total	11.9	13.8	17.9
Men	11.5	12.7	16.3
Women	12.2	15.0	19.2

Source: U.S. National Vital Statistics System, *Federal Interagency Forum on Aging Related Statistics,* www.agingstats...tbook2000/tables-healthstatus.html; *National Vital Statistics Reports, 49,* 12 (2001).

6. A key element in the increase of the aged population is the increasing life expectancy. Life expectancy is how many years more one can expect to live, on average, for a particular age group. One can calculate life expectancy at birth and also for any time after birth. Table 13.2 presents data on life expectancy at birth and life expectancy at age sixty-five. Remember, this means how many more years one can expect to live. Describe the pattern you find for life expectancy for the total population.

7. What are some factors that may help to explain the increasing life expectancy rates?

TABLE 13.3 *Grandchildren Living in the Home of Their Grandparents (in thousands): 1970 to 2000*

Year	Total Children under 18	Living with Grandparents	Percent
1970	69,276	2,214	
1980	63,369	2,306	
1990	64,137	3,155	
2000	72,012	3,842	

Source: U.S. Census Bureau, *Grandchildren Living in the Home of Their Grandparents: 1970 to Present,* release date: June 29, 2001, www.census.gov/population/socdemo/hh-fam/tabCH-7.txt

8. Given the fact that there are larger numbers of the aged population, this increases the possibility that growing numbers of children will have the opportunity to know their grandparents, and also to live with their grandparents. Table 13.3 presents data on grandchildren living in the homes of their grandparents. Calculate the percentage of grandchildren who are living with their grandparents for the years shown and put your answers in the table.

9. Describe the pattern you find in the data.

10. Another way to analyze the data is to calculate the rate of increase for all children under eighteen and children under eighteen living with their grandparents (see question #3). What is the rate of increase for all children?

11. What is the rate of increase for children living with their grandparents?

12. What might account for the increase in the number of children living with their grandparents?

TABLE 13.4   *Grandchildren Living in the Home of their Grandparents by Household Configuration (in thousands): 1970 to 2000*

Household	1970	1980	1990	2000
Total children living with grandparents	2,214	2,306	3,155	3,842
Both parents present	363	310	467	531
% both parents present				
Mother only present	817	922	1,563	1,732
% mother only present				
Father only present	78	86	191	220
% father only present				
No parents present	957	988	935	1,359
% no parents present				

Source: U.S. Census Bureau, *Grandchildren Living in the Home of Their Grandparents: 1970 to Present,* release date: June 29, 2001, www.census.gov/population/socdemo/hh-fam/tabCH-7.txt

13. There can be a number of different household configurations for children living with their grandparents. Their parents may also live in the grandparents' household, creating a three-generation household. The children may be living only with their mother and grandparents, or living only with their father and their grandparents. Lastly, the children may be living with their grandparents without their parents present. Table 13.4 indicates these various configurations. Calculate the percentage distribution by type of household configuration and put your answers in the table.

14. What types of configuration appear to be increasing the fastest?

15. Why do you think these types of configuration are increasing?

16. What issues unique to these types of families might they have to face?

17. How do these patterns you discovered in the data affect your sense of what constitutes a family, or how we come to define families?

Selected Bibliography and Suggested Readings _____

AARP Research Group. (1999). *AARP grandparenting survey: The sharing and caring between mature grandparents and their grandchildren,* November 1999, www. research.aarp.org/general/grandpsurv.html

Cherlin, Andrew, & Furstenberg, Frank. (1992). *The new American grandparent.* Cambridge: Harvard University Press.

De Toledo, Sylvie, & Brown, Deborah. (1995). *Grandparents as parents: A survival guide for raising a second family.* New York: Guilford.

Edelman, Hope. (1999). *Mother of my mother: The intricate bond between generations.* New York: Dial.

Elgin, Suzette. (1998). *The grandmother principles.* New York: Abbeville.

Himes, Christine. (2001, December). Elderly Americans. *Population Bulletin.* Washington, DC: Population Reference Bureau.

Kornhaber, Arthur. (1996). *Contemporary grandparenting.* Thousand Oaks, CA: Sage.

Maugans, J. (1994). *Aging parents, ambivalent baby boomers.* Lanham, MD: AltaMira.

National Committee to Preserve Social Security and Medicare. (2000, February). *Grandparent's guide to navigating the legal system.* Washington, DC.

Price, S., & Brubaker, T. (Eds.). (1996). *Vision 2010: Families and aging.* Minneapolis: National Council on Relations.

Westheimer, Ruth, & Kaplan, Steven. (1998). *Grandparenthood.* New York: Routledge.

Zullo, Kathryn, & Zullo, Alan. (1998). *The nanas and the papas: A boomer's guide to grandparenting.* Kansas City: Andrews McMeel.